TALES FROM THE LOST RIDER OF YAUPON CREEK

By

Herman W. Brune

Illustrated by Tom Stallman

Wild Horse Press

www.WildHorsePress.com

Copyright © 2004
By Herman W. Brune
Published By Wild Horse Press
An Imprint of Wild Horse Media Group
P.O. Box 331779
Fort Worth, Texas 76163
1-817-344-7036
www.WildHorseMedia.com
ALL RIGHTS RESERVED
1 2 3 4 5 6 7 8 9
ISBN-10: 1-68179-091-2
ISBN-13: 978-1-68179-091-6

ACKNOWLEDGEMENTS

I'd like to thank all the folks I've ridden, hunted, and fished with, as well as those who inspired me to write.

DEDICATION

*This book is dedicated to **Samantha Olivia** and **Marjorie Sophia Brune**, my daughter and my mom, the two people who have put up with my wandering ways the most.*

Table of Contents

Foreword

~ Texas ~

~ Mexico ~

~ Montana ~

~ Christmas ~

~ Resorts, Destinations, and Outfitters ~

FOREWORD

Memories are part of the visceral fabric holding our lives together; they're indispensable for learning from experience. Along with genetics, memories are a cornerstone of our personalities. They mold our reasoning and, like safety switches, govern our abilities.

Memories can be positive building blocks to strong relationships and ethereal joy, or they can be strangling snares restricting emotions and stunting happiness. However they appear, it is left to the human intellect to equate the pros and cons and come up with individual solutions effecting the quality of survival.

Mankind, whether bracing real emergencies of family health or the contrived sanctimonious goals assigned by society, rely on deductive thinking, analyzing information, and what they already know in their memories to sustain relative comfort.

Then, enter the wide-open world of the outdoors. Where memories conceive on frosty mornings in duck blinds and deer woods, and splash into our hearts putting a lump in our throat and a fish on the end of our line. They pinch our brains with frozen fingers, stumble on clumsy numb toes, and smack us in the face with moments of personal definition. Then they cloak us in warmth, wrapping us in a warm blanket beside a campfire where we listen to a deep earthly voice and ingest the tutoring of an idolized mentor.

The experiences gathered by people in the outdoors are every bit a part of our education and growth as anything taught in grade school or college.

Writers have been chronicling outdoor stories since man started scratching on the walls of his cave.

The great writers struggle to capture the essence of a moment. They strive to identify the characters, and to introduce the reader to the surroundings and weather. They elaborate the meat of a situation and, in as few words as possible, put the reader into another place and time within an adventure.

The great writers make your skin crawl when whispering of Simba, the lion. They make your nerves tingle when you hear an elk bugle resonate on a clear Rocky Mountain morning. They make you laugh aloud when the rainbow strikes your fly, and they make you blink away tears at the love a quail hunter has for his dog. Then, they fade you deep into the dream of an African safari with giant tusked elephants, walking and lolling their trunks, at the base of Mt. Kilimanjaro.

Today's readers can be transcended to other times and locales by writers such as Twain, Melville, Ruark, Hemingway, and O'Connor.

Robert Ruark was one of the finest writers and disciples of outdoor lesson learning in recent times. He was commonly known as the Poor Man's Hemingway. And while his efforts were comparable to Ernest Hemingway's, the two men were friends.

Taken from Jim Casada's book, *The Lost Classics of Robert Ruark*, Ruark said:

> "But I believe that Hemingway could not have written the bulk of his best without early introduction to rod and rifle. Hemingway had 'it', too, even when 'it' was a secondary theme to a major work. Never had the respect for life and death and the dignity of man been more strikingly shown than in *The Old Man and the Sea*. Hemingway's heroes were mainly simple men and good men, and their instincts were direct and uncomplicated.
>
> It seems to me that we have been losing, and are losing, a great deal of this simplicity of approach to man's natural instincts in a baffling world of

nauseating cant and hypocrisy and contrived complications. We have had so much steam heat and air conditioning that we have forgotten wood fires and fresh air.

It is the fashion of the literati to speak knowingly and loftily of the 'art' of a Hemingway, the 'significance' of a Hemingway, and blandly ignore the fact that he was being neither arty nor sophisticated in most of his writings, but was merely worshipping at the shrine of wood and water, men and women, animals and birds, wine and bread and onions and cheese – worshipping as an antidote to the predestination of all his pieces to end in disaster. Papa gave such people short shrift."

Men and women who make their livings in the outdoors know the teachings and values of life. Their memories and experiences enrich them far more than a fat bank account and comfort them more than a carpeted parlor.

Woe be the CEO of corporate America who lords over a modern-day mule packer bragging about his own business and toys. It will be days before the equine woodsman forgives and honors this wart the consideration of an equal, and only then after the pagan has humbled himself and proves he has an honest human heart.

This book is meant to enjoy, and maybe accidentally give some insights everyone can relate to. It is full of neighbors, friends, and folks I've laughed with while guiding on hunts from Mexico to Montana.

I have no false illusions or desires to add my name to any lists of great writers. They suffered too many personal torments and too often died in untimely fashions.

However, I would like to point out the difference between myself and the outdoor technical experts who expound the where-tos, when-tos, why-tos, and how-tos of calling an elk, or skinning a buck, or plucking a duck, or hooking a bass on the latest loopty-dee-doo-top-poppin'-battery - operated-dooma-ka-jiggy-your-wife-will-like-it too, fishing lure.

I don't wear much camo, and I'm a fan of old lever guns, single action pistols, and bowie knives. Nowadays, I ride saddles with association trees and a roping horn. I'm too old to change much, but I hope I'm never too constipated to accept or share a good idea.

And with that thought, please, understand that these tales are cherished memories and lessons offered to you – as honestly and openly and straight from the heart as a cowboy can give.

~ T E X A S ~

Smiley

S miley came to live with me in the spring of 1986. He needed a place to camp and offered to help build fence, work cows, or break horses. I needed good help and welcomed some cowboy company. I never knew where he came from, and it seemed impolite to ask.

It's not the western code to ask personal questions when somebody is offering their assistance.

He was an unassuming quiet-type gentleman. An easy smile and a self-confident style of working were his trademarks. He was one of those types who always seemed to be in the right place at the right time doing what needed to be done.

Through the years we became steadfast friends, and once or twice had to pull each other out of a mess.

Some mornings he'd show up with one of his sheepish I-just-got-out-of-jail grins smattered across his face. I worried about him a little, but not too much. I knew his taste in females was questionable; and I never doubted that he had any qualms about dating more than one at a time. My concern was that he'd run into some poisonous ol' pedigreed hide who would get him shot.

However in true cowboy fashion, his love for horses exonerated him from transgressions. He preferred a cowpony to human company any time.

He was also living proof that common sense, good work ethics, and instincts are worth more than a college degree. I noticed many times, when I had company at the house, that Smiley was the smartest one in the crowd.

He wasn't a big drinker. He wouldn't touch hard liquor and would only take a few sips of beer. That was probably the most un-cowboy thing about him.

Hunting was not one of his main loves, and fishing was something that confounded him. Nevertheless, he begged me to take him along on a pack trip to Montana in 1993. I took him and he practically froze his tail off, but he never complained. All he did was smile. It was –22 degrees the morning we headed back for Texas, and he swore that once he got home he'd never leave again.

He hated coyotes and loved to fight bad cows. He was the best cow-penning help I ever had, but he was sort of sensitive. We worked well as a team but any time somebody else came along I could tell he was perturbed. The problem was compounded if they talked to him. Numerous times he quit and went back to the truck to sulk because some novice cowpuncher hollered at him. One hundred percent of the time he was right. If a person kept their mouth shut and watched him – he was always in the right place making the right moves. Not many people were smart enough to learn from him.

His sensitivity caused me to protect him from folks with bad manners.

He disliked loud noises and hated it when the wind blew the rumbling from the Glidden train-yards our direction. He liked shooting even less. Smiley would either go across the road to mom's house, or up to the beer joint whenever there was a shooting match on my range.

I often warned him about getting hit by a beer truck but he'd just smile and ignore me.

Despite his aversion to high decibels he did like Creedence Clearwater Revival and Lynyrd Skynyrd. He'd throw a little dance into his walk whenever he'd hear the Midnight Special or Sweet Home Alabama.

He took good care of my daughter, Sam, and would periodically wander across the road to check on my mom. The family loved him. Everybody loved him. Rain or shine he always had a smile for everyone.

He was the subject of an essay that I had to write when taking a spelling, grammar, and punctuation test at Texas A&M University.

Smiley wore his heart on his sleeve. He showed his affections. He showed his anger.

He wasn't a good fighter; but he wouldn't back down from the devil. He was always loyal, and always handy.

The last couple of years his hips began degenerating and I had to help him in and out of the truck. His bottom eyelids started hanging in a droopy watery way, and his bottom lip began to sag. He always had a thank-you-boss look on his face. His ribs began to stick out, and I could tell that his sight and hearing were failing him. But he never quit smiling, and he'd always limp along and help me with my chores.

Several times I caught him looking at me, and his eyes peered into me and told me that the end would be coming soon – I could feel him saying goodbye.

Then one day he was gone. I didn't know that his time was already up. I'd hoped he'd be around a little longer.

He wandered out of my life the way he wandered into it. I don't know where he went to die. I never found him. He went off to be alone and to pass away in peace without a lot of fuss.

I often teased myself with the belief that Smiley was a western-man reincarnated and sent to help me. He helped me through some hard years.

In the end, he left me one of his sons to carry on his job.

Now, I hope that when my time comes – I can leave without a fuss, and there will be a smiling speckled dog meeting me when I ride up to the Gates.

Dad's Daydream

The church crowd invaded the barbecue restaurant in synchronized waves. Several of the men were slim, wore white straw hats, white shirts, western dress pants, and cowboy boots. Their faces were lined and tan, their shirtsleeves were rolled up their sunburned arms to their elbows. The other men were pink-faced and bulbous-shaped with their jowls hanging over tight-buttoned collars, sweating in the gulf coast humidity but still wearing neckties. All the ladies sported flowery Sunday dresses, sprayed hairdos, and too much jewelry. It was a classic Norman Rockwell scene from rural Texas.

I looked at my daughter. The two of us were alone at our table.

"I think we got our food just in time," I said.

Mounted white-tailed and mule deer, elk, wild hogs, black bear, and moose heads bedecked the interior of the restaurant. There were also many exotic mounts. Blackbuck antelope, fallow and axis deer, eland, kudu, and cape buffalo finished filling out practically every inch of the rough-planked walls. It provided the room a gaudy décor – but individually each piece of taxidermy was unique and offered a different, silent story.

A family scattered around the table near us. Two cotton-top boys took seats beside their dad. The mother took the chair across from her husband. He was in his mid-40s, about five-foot-ten inches tall, and 200 pounds – his lunch muscles were beginning to show. Dressed in contemporary casual attire he was a new generation Texan, adept to the computer age but familiar with old traditions. He sat down, looked up onto the wall, and his mind seemed to slip into another world.

I watched him.

The children jabbered beside him, and his wife began to say something and then stopped. She saw he wasn't listening. A mounted moose head hypnotized him. She studied his face for a moment and with a quiet nod turned her attention to the boys. She decided to let her man dream.

He was lost.

Perhaps his mind had found an old file where Jack O'Connor and Robert Ruark chronicled wilderness mountain adventures in eloquent prose. Their audiences transcended dull suffocating lifestyles to imagine wall-tented camps, hunting horseback in clean high country air, bugling elk, and quartered game hanging on the meat pole.

I smiled and turned to peer at the other patrons. In the center of the dining room was a man pointing to a mount and discussing it with his teenage son. On the far side was another gentleman, his consciousness averted above the crowd, he'd succumbed to the trance of a gigantic whitetail.

Then I glanced back at the first man and the moose head that had captured his good sense. For a moment I wished I could see the country where such animals lived.

Then a bolt of reality hit me – I had.

Soggy wet melting snow soaked through my old boots and saturated my socks. My gloves were equally useless and my fingers throbbed. Old bronc-riding injuries and the aching cold hurt my knees as I limped toward the tents frowning and looking for problems. The early elk season started the next day and I wanted my hunters to be comfortable and ready. I knew how to pack mules and guide, but it was the first time I was responsible for managing an outfitter's camp. My other hunting guide was a mule packer who had never guided before and my cook was a big-eared college kid who had never been to the mountains without his daddy. I was worried.

Camp occupied a diminutive grassy meadow at the head of Strawberry Creek in the Bob Marshall Wilderness. It was a small set-up, but efficient and tidy. Three canvas-walled tents served as a cook tent, a hunter's tent, and a crew tent. There was also a set of corrals and a flagpole with the Lone Star flag fluttering in the breeze signaling my pride in wild Montana. We were 14 miles horseback from the truck, and the truck was 50 miles from town. Our supplies were packed in on mules. An adequate quantity of firewood was bucked-up and stacked. Satisfied for the moment, I relaxed and enjoyed the warmth of the cook tent and the excitement of the hunters.

They went to sleep that night burrowed into their bedrolls, listening to pine knots cracking in the wood stove, and murmuring expectations for the next day's hunt.

I rolled out in the early a.m. It was pitch dark. I kicked the cook's bunk and sent him to prepare breakfast. The weather was warm and all the snow was gone. I fired up a lantern and hung it on a hook by the corrals. The other guide joined me and we started saddling. I wanted to be on the ridge above camp at daylight.

The hunters wolfed down breakfast, arranged their gear, and got situated on their horses. The other guide took two hunters and headed down the creek. I took two, and trusting my horse to stay on the trail, rode up through the black timber.

The timing was perfect. An hour later, we stood on the ridge listening to bull elk bugle in three different directions while our eyes adjusted to the slow dawn. I pinpointed the closest bull. Then I put one of my hunters on a heavily used trail that crossed between two alpine basins. The other hunter and I took off towards the bellowing calls of the herd bull.

We hustled up a hill stressing the limits of our endurance, then slowed as we passed over the crest.

Our pace became a hunched-over creep and finally we crawled to look on the far side of the slope. Below us a dozen cow elk grazed unaware of our presence.

I moved my man to a log where he could be prone, rest his rifle, and have a clear view. We watched the cows in awe, knowing we were enjoying a special day in our lives. In a moment the bull strode out of a timbered draw. My hunter flipped his rifle's safety off, nestled the gun into his shoulder, and concentrated through the scope. I appreciated the animal through my binoculars and observed as the shot did its duty.

Then the clouds rolled in and started dumping snow. By the time I had the elk caped and dressed there was a blanket of snow covering everything.

After that, my plans fell short. The other hunters fumbled two more chances at elk. Nevertheless, it was a happy camp. The crew worked hard, and the clients were a friendly set of guys – even if they weren't good shots.

The weather remained cold throughout the week, and on the last evening it turned drizzly and began to snow again.

The hunt was over, and we were all in the cook tent sipping Canadian anti-freeze when I heard my bell mares stampede. We rushed to see what was causing the ruckus.

There in the middle of camp was a bull moose! He was waging war against a small pine tree with his antlers and making love-talk to my mare mules. However, they were having none of it and headed for the timber. We admired him for awhile, then began cussing and chunking snowballs at him – to run him off.

The next morning we were missing two mules. I shuffled pack loads and riders; then leading my packstring, I walked over Birch Creek Pass, out of the mountains, and back to the truck.

My head rocked back and my mind reeled into the present. I was staring wide-eyed and locked on the moose head hanging on the restaurant wall.

I glanced at the other dreamer. He blinked and looked around with a numb vacant expression, then rejoined his family for lunch.

My daughter was studying me from across the table and smiling. I winked at her and stabbed a piece of barbecue with my fork.

Saltwater Gets Into Everything, Even Your Blood

"Saltwater Gets Into Everything, Even Your Blood" won first place in the Texas Outdoor Writers Association's Excellence in Craft awards for Humor in a publication with a circulation under 25,000.

I hate getting wet. I was the kind of baby that bellered and squalled while mama poured soapy water over my head and bathed me in the sink. There is something creepy and unnatural about being wet all over. To have the entire surface area of your body immersed in suffocating water seems unhealthy.

Some scientist said that man evolved from creatures of the sea – which makes perfect sense. It's easy to believe a critter would be smart enough to crawl out of the ocean and quit drowning.

History tells us more cowboys died in the 1800s crossing rivers than from gunfights. So, I think it is reasonable for me to have a distaste for dampness. I once went 21 days in a Montana hunting camp without a bath. I understand how the old timers put on a pair of longhandles in the fall and cut them off in the spring. I hate getting wet.

The only thing worse than being wet is being ignorant.

- Galveston State Park

My assignment for the Texas A&M Recreation and Parks Tourism Science class was to do an outdoor activity that I'd never done before. We were given a list of possibilities; I studied it. At my age there is, little I haven't done, but midway down the list I saw a weekend "Sea Kayaking" trip.

After a dreary winter of feeding cows, a trip to the coast sounded like fun. I was sure I'd never kayaked in the ocean. The closest thing I'd ever done to kayaking was during the Great Colorado County Canoe Race. Space Monkey Girndt and I rooster-tailed down the Colorado River and beat Leonard Boettcher and Scott Gorman like a couple of tongue-tied donkey-riding stepchildren.

Now, my confidence was washing away.

I stood there looking at Galveston Bay and my old fears flooded back to me. The waves and continuous splashing of the surf made my head spin. I found myself grinding my teeth and clenching my fists. My nerves felt sloshed. It seemed impossible for a person to swim in that much water. It was too big. It would swallow me.

Bulbous jellyfish lay scattered along the beach like exposed aquatic land mines; and I thought about the other meat-eating, gilled critters hiding in the tomb of the bay's dark water. I assume that after a landlubber drowns there are plenty of sea-coyotes and fishy, turkey buzzards to clean up the carcass.

Then I thought about sharks. Dadgum... Signs warn about rattlesnakes on the sand dunes, and when you get in the water you have to fret about sharks.

Wait a minute... I can tolerate being nervous for only so long. Then I clamp my molars and start claiming real estate. A shark is just a fishy kind of grizzly bear. Some folks pay a lot of money for sharkskin boots. My brain clicked into its big game mode and put everything into perspective. I dug out my pocketknife. It was butter knife dull. Then I checked the Puma folding knife on my belt. It was sharp enough to trim chin whiskers. Yeah, let ol' toothy-fishy get sassy. I'll stretch his hide on the barn wall and make me a new pair of boots.

I started to feel a little better.

The group of kids with the Texas A&M Outdoors Department showed up and pitched camp after dark. There were 10 of them in a van, and they towed a trailer load of kayaks.

I realize I don't know squat about anything once I get on the south side of Interstate 10. The Coastal Plain and its bird hunting are a mystery to me. The beach communities are confounding. I'm out of my realm of expertise. My opinions are based on assumption. Everything has a coat of salt on it, and even the people have strange habits.

The folks along the coast dress like poor people. They look like they're from a third world country. They like to wear raggedy t-shirts and short pants. Most of the time they're either bare-footed or wearing footwear they found at the dump. They're sunburned and squinty eyed like starved moles. Their fried, frizzled stick-like hair pokes out from under nondescript ball caps like its trying to escape. They live in houses on stilts. I'm guessing that after standing at sea level all day they need an altitude change. This is a natural reaction associated with humans' instincts to move to higher ground. It also helps them see farther and is a measure of social status. Whoever has the highest house can see farthest and has more money than the neighbors. Sometimes an inch is all it takes to be on the next rung of the social ladder allowing that person to hold their nose a little higher.

Meanwhile, our camp was peaceful and I rolled up in my bedroll under the stars. I looked up at some constellations like they were old buddies, and had a nice snooze.

The next morning was great. If you ever want to start your day right, listen to young people. They gush exuberance and excitement. The trials and tribulations of the heathen business world hasn't jaded them. They don't notice pain.

We headed to an inland beach.

I'm guessing that "kayak" is a Japanese word for long skinny plastic boat. They're not very big, so they don't get saddled with a big name. "Kayak" fits them about right. They're not wide enough, so they can be a little tippy until you plant your bottomside firm in the seat.

One of the students gave a short talk on the operation of the vehicle, and then we scattered out to find our mounts.

I screwed my big straw cowboy hat down tight, took hold of my boat, and headed straight into the Gulf of Mexico. There was no way to crawl on without getting wet. I hunted a stirrup and finally jumped on bareback. Now, I found two problems.

Those plastic boats have holes in the bottom – for no reason at all! The holes let water in and the seat is underwater. When I swung aboard my backside landed square in a puddle. My eyes bugged out and my teeth hurt. I almost bellered. I don't think a sudden dose of saltwater is good for hemorrhoids.

At the same instant, my plastic boat went to sunfishing and trying to pitch. But he wasn't the toughest thing I'd ever crawled on, and soon I had him settled down and lined out. In a minute we were cutting the waves and I was trying to remember a couple of sailor songs.

We took off as a group to circle Mud Island. I felt like Tom Selleck on Magnum PI. Folks confuse me for Tom Selleck all the time. I could imagine a dozen bikini-clad beauties running along the beach calling, "Tom, Tom, or Herman, Herman ...pick me, pick me." However, when I glanced at the beach all I saw was a congregation of squawking sea gulls.

The rest of the trip became an outdoor classroom fascination. We identified birds and enjoyed each other's company.

Our student guide proclaimed his desire to be an outdoor writer, and I beseeched him to drown himself.

I eventually got used to sitting in the saltwater, and even considered its therapeutic qualities. I tried to figure how a guy could enjoy sitting in saltwater while watching television.

The weekend went too fast. Our camp was filled with good feelings. Standing beside the ocean became as natural as walking along a backwoods trail in the wilderness.

The morals to this conglomeration of foolishness are:

Don't ever be scared to try something new, especially if there is the chance that you will make new friends while you're doing it.

And, you can't always look cool while you're having real fun – sitting in a puddle.

Chasing the Pigskin
with the Pros

Everyone stood silent, concentrating, listening, and looking at each other from furrowed brows. Then there was a faint sound. In one motion everyone's arms went into the air pointing toward the distant baying of the dogs. "There!"

We scrambled back into Ty Detmer's hunting truck and rumbled across the pasture towards the fracas-in-progress. As we neared, our anxiety burned into a fever. Our desire to get into the fight became overwhelming. We bailed out of the truck and hit the brush running.

Chris Ruhman, offensive tackle for the Cleveland Browns, followed me. A maze of game trails channeled us toward the battle. Suddenly there were black pigs running everywhere. The hounds had cornered a litter. As we approached, each little pig squealed and ran a different direction. My head snapped from side to side trying to make sense of the commotion.

Then a 20-pound wannabe Russian boar came trotting down the trail toward me. He was snapping his teeth and acting mad at the world, just the way the big hogs do. I grinned and started to figure how to catch the little runt. Within six feet of me, he stopped realizing that danger lay ahead. He hesitated. The dogs were howling behind him, and I was in front of him. In a flash, his little piggy brain made a decision and he bolted my way. With a whoop, I dove at him – and missed. He went between my legs like a slippery fumble. Spinning around in the dirt I turned to see if Chris would catch him.

Horror filled Chris' eyes, his mouth dropped open and he raised his .357 hand-cannon. I was too close to the action. In a heartbeat, there was a lot of yelling and a lot of shooting. I scrambled the opposite direction, into the brush, looking for a hole. When the dust settled, I poked my head out and eased out of my hiding spot.

Sonny Detmer and his son Ty were laughing when we got there.

"I saw my whole career flash before my eyes when that wild hog attacked me," Chris said.

Sonny smiled and looked at me. "How big was that hog, Herman?"

I held my hands about a foot apart, and everyone laughed again. "Dang near shot the guide," I said.

We loaded back into the truck and went to the ranch house for breakfast.

I know first-hand why linemen don't get to handle the pigskin. They're scared of it.

De-ja vu Brings a Gurgle and a Smile

It happened too fast. The deceitful heifer dashed through the brush and down the creek bank holding her tail in the air. She followed a cow trail up the opposite bank and vanished into a yaupon thicket. I raced a short distance behind riding my favorite horse, Dusty.

We leaped from the top of the bank and landed in the soft creek bed. In an instant, I saw a way to head off the errant escaper and jerked my horse to the side. The sudden change of direction made him stumble. He lunged and tried to get his feet back under himself but we'd jumped into loose sand beside a deep water hole and he floundered. The sandbar sloped fast into the water and our momentum carried us in. Dusty fell and rolled. I went under him with my foot hung in the stirrup. I was pinned – underwater. My nerves held until the second my head submerged, then I began to fight. I'd already chunked the reins and flopped to my belly to get away. Dusty was scrambling to get up and I kicked with my free foot at the seat of the saddle. Then we were apart.

Instincts, or my guardian angel, brought me back to the surface and guided me. In a moment I was crawling back onto the sandbar. I collapsed there – drenched, panting, and trying to get over my fear. Then, through a fog, my mind showed me the last time I'd laid on a bank gasping and wheezing.

We were kids. I was past the age of being cute and caught in the awkward stage when little boys are plain dumb. Carol Hanak, Dana Girndt, and Sandy Rhodes climbed the ladder to the high board. I sat on the edge of the pool admiring more than the sunny day. They went one at a time and executed perfect one-and-a-half somersaults, diving headfirst without making a splash.

I was afraid of the high board, but I saw a chance to make an impression. So, I gathered all my courage and made a try. I jumped, cut a flip, and landed flat on my face. In those days I couldn't tread water. I dog paddled back to the edge, to keep from sinking to the bottom, and looked around to see if anyone had noticed. My face burned red for more than one reason.

The three girls had their backs to me and were climbing back up the ladder. One – two – three – they each dove from the sky like beautiful young swans, did one-and-a-half somersaults, and glided through the crystal water.

My pride was hurt. Obviously, no one had watched my first effort and I needed to show my manly courage again. This time I bounced higher, flipped harder, and landed with a splat that got almost everyone's attention. My entire front side stung, the air was knocked out of me, and it took me awhile to dog paddle back to the edge.

That was enough. I couldn't do it again. I looked around once more to see the girls' reactions but they didn't know I was alive. It seemed as if they made a conscious effort not to notice me, like I was contagious and if they looked at me it might cause acne or warts.

Then they went back up the ladder to the high board. I marveled at them. They were magnificent. In turns, each of them took two steps and sprang from the board. For an instant they silhouetted motionless against the clear sky stretched in an arcing dive, then somersaulted one-and-a-half times, and slid beneath the surface like icy blades slicing through silk.

Then they laughed and chattered as they swam to the side and exited, walking down the edge of the pool and ignoring me like a toad.

I was crushed. But something made me try one more time. Now, I was just doing it for me.

I took two steps, bounced as high as I could, cut a flip, and never came close to completing the dive. I hit flat and hard. All the air smacked out of my body and I hurt from the top of my head to my toes. It took too long for me to quit sinking and start dog paddling. I came to the top sucking for air and struggling to get my abused body to functioning. I was addled and paddled in circles for a few seconds spitting and gagging before I finally lined out and headed for the bank. A couple of snickering kids helped me out of the pool and I lay on the bank gasping and wheezing.

The memory made me chuckle and smile. My breathing was coming easier. I pulled off my boots and emptied the water out of them, then pulled them back on. Dusty was standing a short distance off, his reins tangled in the brush. I stood up and wiped the wet sand and gravel from my clothes and moved to catch him.

As I walked, I wondered at the different paths my friends' lives have taken since childhood. And I wondered at the individual fears we all had to overcome. I hope we all smile at the memories.

Then my thoughts turned to catching the deceitful heifer.

Summer Days
Are Made For Kids

K eith Schobel walked wide circles around me. He wouldn't
come close.

"C'mon, it's just a little spider," I said.

"I don't like spiders!" he said.

"Aw, well, I don't like snakes – so we're even. If we see a
snake you kill it and if we see a spider I'll kill it."

I was trying to lull him into a false sense of security, but Keith
knew me too well and stayed away.

Finally, I gave up. It was too hot to play silly games and I was
standing in the middle of a prairie, in a hand-dug hole, with work
to do. Gophers were taking over the whole country and I had to
stop them. They had started at grandma's garden. The measly little
rodents dug mounds between the potato and carrot rows. Me and
my gopher traps were all that stood between starvation and having
enough vegetables put up for the winter.

"Herman Willie, I'll give you ten cents for every gopher you catch," said grandma. "And I'll go to Seymour's and buy you some more traps."

Grandma was good about buying hunting supplies. She kept me stocked in Peter's .22 bullets for my never-ending crusades against armadillos. Now, she was putting me in a real business.

She had four or five rusty old gopher traps, but for my endeavors, I was going to need a half-dozen more. Grandma didn't immediately grasp the extent of my entrepreneurial dreams.

In a week I had all the vermin eradicated from the gravel hilltop of the Brune estate. However, it made good sense that in order to keep the problem under control I'd need to widen my trapping circles. Besides, I felt like I had an open-ended contract.

By the second week, I was digging holes and sliding my traps into gopher tunnels along Yaupon Creek. I was also stretching my lines the opposite direction and had traps set in my mama's front yard. The trapline was so extensive I had to put up white undershirt flags on broomsticks to find my sets.

By the third week, the chore had become so labor intensive I needed some help. There was too much equipment for one little boy to drag around. I had ten traps and they were anchored with wire to short boards in sets of twos. Then I had more short boards to use for plugs over the tunnels where traps were set. If a gopher can see daylight shining into his tunnel from a couple of feet underground – even a dadgum gopher isn't that stupid – he'll abandon the use of that tunnel. I also had to pack along a sharpshooter shovel, a grubbing hoe, and my flagging stuff. A red wagon solved part of the transportation problem, but it didn't completely satisfy my labor concerns. So, I employed Keith Schobel, the neighbor boy.

However, he did not realize that fear of spiders could result in the forfeiture of any expected wages or profit sharing.

Now, I stood waist deep in a little boy's hole in the middle of the prairie. Keith wouldn't come close to me and I wondered what a spider was doing, in a gopher hole, out here in the middle of nowhere. Sand and dirt caked my hands, arms, and face. Sweat turned it to sludge. My hair was full of grit inside my bent straw hat. The summer sun baked me along with the surrounding countryside. Even the goatweeds and bullnettle were suffering.

"How far you reckon we are from the house?" I asked.

"Shoot, we gotta be a half-mile," Keith said.

"You reckon a gopher travels that far?"

"I don't know."

"How would a gopher know where grandma's garden is from this far away?"

"I don't know."

My low quarter shoes were full of dirt and I sat on the edge of the hole and emptied them one at a time.

"I'm getting tired of digging. What do you want to do this evening?" I asked.

"Let's go fishing in Ms. Willie Mae's tank."

"The big tank?" I asked.

"Yeah."

I knew Keith's dad had some mongo fishing worms, under a sheet of tin, beside their septic line.

"You got enough worms for both of us?" I asked.

"No ! You gotta bring your own."

That dadgum Keith was always ornery that way – wish I could find that spider.

Growing Pains

O ne of the old sheriff's favorite sayings was to ask me if I was behaving. When I affirmed that I was indeed being a pious citizen he'd chuckle and say, "Well, then you ain't having no fun."

Rusty and I were experts on having fun.

We left the '53 GMC pickup at the foot of the hill, and snuck towards the house with armloads of soft white huggable rolls of ammunition. We knew that success depended upon Indian-style stealth and silence as well as dumb luck. I was glad that it was a dark night.

The lights from the living room shined across the front porch and provided faint illumination into the front yard. We kept an eye on the house and began wrapping the smaller trees. It didn't take long. Our fear kept us from getting too close to the front porch and out of the light coming directly from the windows. The little good sense we had told us to start at a point nearest the house and work our way away from it.

We wrapped the smaller trees, and when we thought they had enough toilet paper on them, we gave them some more. As we worked and neared the completion of our chore, we became braver. We left long streamers lying across the yard and then sent three or four rolls flying, and tailing 20 feet of Charmin, into the big oak trees at the ends of the driveway.

By the time we were through, we were retching and shaking with the giggles. Nobody had ever wrapped Harvey Lee's house.

We trotted back down the hill, cranked up the truck, and puttered towards town. It had been a quick adventure, and we figured Mr. Harvey would see the humor in it. We also knew he would warn us about Ms. Hilda shooting no-count renegades like ourselves.

We loved Harvey Lee.

The Brunes and the Lees were always good friends. Mr. Harvey hunted with great uncle Monroe Kuhn and my grandpa Herman Brune Jr. I never knew my grandfather, so I hung on every word that Mr. Harvey said about him. I hung on every word he said anyway. I idolized the man.

He was a big man, black-headed, dark-tanned, square-jawed, hard as iron, and in shape to take on whatever the world threw at him. His hands were twice the size of most men's, and when he rolled them into fists he seemed bigger than life. He was the youngest sheriff in Texas.

He was a western man. I believed all the wild-west stories he told me. He taught me the standards that a man needed to live by to have honor. He helped me grow up, and made it okay to be a kid.

He had his detractors, but I always figured those folks were jealous. I decided a long time ago what I was going to believe.

The lessons I learned from him are with me everyday. The echo of his voice is right there with grandma's, and daddy's, and those folks that have gone on.

We wrapped Mr. Harvey's house and I took Rusty home. I was hungry and still looking for excitement so I headed to town.

As I pulled up in front of the cafe, I was surprised to see Mr. Harvey's '77 Chevy pickup.

Shoot – we had been so sneaky, and the whole time he was playing 42 in the domino hall.

I parked behind the Chevy and had a bright idea. These new trucks had easy-to-take-off tailgates. So... I detached his tailgate and laid it in the bed of my truck.

I walked into Busselman's cafe snickering and thinking that soon Mr. Harvey would join me for a cup of coffee.

However, I had a glass of tea, ate a burger and fries, and when I went out again he was gone.

Doubt about my joke crossed my mind but I was past worrying.

The next morning, about eight o'clock, I drove back into town. There was his pickup in the same parking spot it was in the night before.

I parked behind it again, took his tailgate out of the bed of my truck, and put it back on his truck.

Then I ambled peacefully and stupidly over to the domino hall.

When I entered, he was talking to chief of police, Tom Wine.

"Yes sir, some durn rascal swiped my tailgate while I was in here playing dominoes last night," Mr. Harvey said.

Then he saw me.

"Come here boy, I want to show you."

He caught me by the arm, turned me around, and walked me back out of the domino hall as he continued his narrative of the missing tailgate. He pointed at his truck across the street.

Tom Wine looked across the street, saw the tailgate, saw my truck, looked back at me, and evaporated from the scene.

Mr. Harvey continued to point at his truck but began stuttering and stumbling over the next couple of words in his story.

Then he got quiet.

His jaw seemed to tighten and set as he looked at his tailgate and the two trucks parked across the street.

His brow became heavy. He had an earnest look on his face. He stood there, bowlegged with a slight hunch in his shoulders, clenching and unclenching his hands in front of himself. Then he turned so he could look straight at me.

"Uh-oh."

A Tale of Two Stories

"A Tale of Two Stories" won a national award in the Outdoor Writers Association of America's 2001, newspaper humor writing contest division.

Rusty's Story:

You ain't going to believe what the old man made me do.

We pulled up to the dock in Palacios. It was about an hour before dark and the tide had gone out. We had a mess of fish to clean and we still needed to set up our cots. We were going to sleep on the beach.

I jumped up on the dock and tied the boat. Daddy was doodling around and started handing me stuff. He set his filet knife on top of a cooler, and then grabbed it by the handles to set it out of the boat. Well, his knife slid off and fell into the water.

You should have seen him, he stood there with his mouth hanging open. I thought he was going to cry. That was his favorite fish cleaning knife. He couldn't talk for a little while... then he went to cussing.

I just figured that knife was gone. Hell, it was a four-dollar Wal-Mart knife. Go buy another one. But the first words out of his mouth were, "How am I going to get my knife back?"

I told him to forget it. There wasn't no way. That knife fell in eight-foot of water.

But he wouldn't let it go. He got nervous and was muttering to himself the whole time we cleaned fish. He ran through a half dozen plans trying to figure a way to get his knife.

He kept fretting while we set up cots, and then I could hear him tossing, turning most of the night. He aggravated himself so bad worrying about getting that damn knife back that he couldn't sleep.

I said to hell with it, drank a few beers, and listened to the waves. It was sort of funny watching him fuss with himself. I figured we'd go fishing in the morning and he'd be over it.

Well it wasn't so durn funny the next morning when he was grinning at me saying he knew how to get his knife back.

He kept a 10-foot piece of metal conduit in the boat, and he poked it to the bottom where he figured the knife should be. Then he looked at me and said "you crawl down this pipe and feel around 'til you find my knife."

I couldn't believe it. I thought he was kidding. The tide had come in and out, and there was no telling what kind of trash everybody else had dropped in that spot. On top of that, it was cold

– it wasn't swimming weather. But he was dead serious. He was even smiling a little, just thinking about getting his knife back.

I shook my head in disbelief. I took my clothes off. I couldn't believe he was asking me to do this. I couldn't believe I was doing it.

I eased into the freezing gunky water and lost my breath to the cold. Then put one hand on the conduit, sucked in a bunch of wind, and slid down the pipe to the bottom. It was like jumping into your toilet bowl and feeling around on the bottom to see what you can find.

I squatted on the bottom and held on to the pipe, then felt my way in a circle. I duck-walked around the pipe holding my breath. I just knew I'd get a treble-hook in a bare foot any minute.

I dived three times, each time feeling a little farther from the pipe. The last time I was stretched out as far as I could reach, and like magic my hand closed around the knife.

Daddy was so happy. I just couldn't believe the whole crazy mess. I was soaking wet and turning blue. He was ready to go fishing again – old fart.

Raymond's Story:

My knife fell in the water and Rusty just about had a fit. I don't know why he got so upset. It was an old cheap wore-out knife from Wal-Mart. Hell, I could get another one for a couple of bucks.

But Rusty was going nuts. Losing that knife for me upset him terrible. I thought he was going to cry.

I told him not to worry about it, but that didn't help. He worried all night. I heard him talking and turning and grumbling. I don't think he slept at all.

But the next morning he said he'd figured out how to get my knife back. He wanted to go diving for it.

I argued with him, I thought it was a bad idea. The tide had gone in and out, and there was no telling what kind of trash was on the bottom next to a dock.

But he wouldn't listen. I couldn't talk him out of it. He took his clothes off, stuck that conduit in the bottom about where he thought the knife ought to be, and told me to hold it. Then he bailed in like Lloyd Bridges going on a "Sea Hunt." I never seen him so excited about doing something.

And you know what? – third time down we found it! I was surprised!

I never figured we'd find that durn thing.

I'm mighty proud of him. He hopped out of the water and was ready to go back to fishing.

- Raymond passed away a few years ago, but Rusty and I live with some wonderful memories of enjoying the outdoors with him. Now, I'm looking at Rusty's boys trying to guess which one will be a diver for us someday.

An Impossible Task Made Possible by a Friend

The wind tugged at my straw cowboy hat as the old aluminum boat cut its way through Oyster Lake. The flat bottom boat didn't slide or glide. It was equivalent to riding a Willis jeep across the pasture to a deer stand.

A teenage smile reflected my exuberance. It creased my face, threw light into my eyes, and extended to a place where it was rooted inside me. If someone dipped into my adolescent think tank they would discover a net full of wet squiggly little tadpole ideas. Their most significant redeeming value being they were strong swimmers.

Mr. Raymond Klaus, my best friend Rusty's dad, aimed the gray metal boat at the saltwater lake. He knew the tricky trail that wound through the shallows – or at least he said he did. Occasionally the propeller dug into the mucky oyster shell bottom and we'd jolt to a stop. Then he'd raise the motor, look to see if the prop was still there, inspect the damage, cuss like a carpenter gone fishing, put the prop down, position me on the front of the boat, pull the starter rope, and we'd plow ahead.

We eventually snuck out a corner of the lake into the intercoastal canal, and Mr. Raymond's confidence returned. He cranked the throttle and his sturdy scow bounced on top of the water like an ATV racing across a rice field. I could feel the old man's happiness without looking at him. We sailed on with him running the motor and me perched on the front. Both of us, our heads high in the wind, anticipating a great day of catching fish. At my age, all my days were great.

Mr. Raymond was a tad-bit proud about his fishing skills. He always expected to catch the first fish, the most fish, and the biggest fish – he always did. I wasn't even competition. His standard tradition was to get his line in the water first, and as his cork settled he'd announce, "Okay, ready on this end!"

I didn't have enough sense to get ready before we stopped. He'd be fishing while I fiddled with knots and tried to find my hooks, leaders, corks, and the perfect shrimp for bait.

We eased to a halt where the canal sideswiped the back of the lake. His intention was to fish a point where the shallows dropped off into the canal. It was a favorite spot.

Rusty didn't make this trip. It was my sole responsibility to try and keep up with the old man.

Mr. Raymond planted the anchor and let the boat turn in the wind. I looked at our location and thought we were still too far from the drop-off. I watched as he made his first cast. It kited long and straight. The cork straightened in the salty water and bobbed on the low waves, never seeming to be an intruder to the bay's natural life. It remained silent for only seconds. Then it jerked beneath the surface and the old fisherman exclaimed, "You better get out there if you want to catch fish!"

My fumbling became frantic. He had a speckled trout in the ice cooler by the time I made my first cast.

I heaved my line skyward toward the unsuspecting school of trout – and it fell short. Meanwhile, Mr. Raymond's next cast was true and in a moment he was reeling in another keeper. I watched my cork. It floated dejected and lonesome like a piece of trash lost on the water. Then I reeled it in and cast again. This time I put my back into it – short again.

My idea of proper reel maintenance was to spray WD-40 into my Zebco 202. Now, I was getting my first taste of an equipment battle.

Mr. Raymond caught another one, and I tried to put more muscle behind each cast. He began to revel in the moment and snicker in a nasal voice.

"Heh, heh, heh, yeah this is a good spot. I always catch fish when I come here," he said.

I studied the situation.

"Why don't we pick up the anchor and drift in a little closer so I can reach them?" I asked.

"Oh no, can't do that. We might spook them off. Heh, heh, heh."

My spirits dropped and I had some mean thoughts. Then I turned around and started fishing on the other side of the boat.

Mr. Raymond kept hooking trout, and had to throw a bunch of little ones back. The honey-hole lasted until noon and finally petered out. By now, I was napping.

"Want some lunch?" he asked.

"Sure, are you going to pull over to the bank?" I asked.

"Shoot no, there's rattlesnakes on the bank," he said.

There was no pulling over to the bank on these coastal trips. This made for particular hardships when the call of nature arrived. A five-gallon bucket was kept available for these purposes. This isn't a major problem for the guys, but since this trip I've had two ex-wives who had to use the bucket. They each made only one fishing trip with us.

"Tell you what, let's go out Half-Moon Reef after lunch," Mr. Raymond said.

"Okay, but you've got two extra rods in here that you ain't using. I'd like to use one of them this afternoon," I said.

He growled and agreed. "You can use this Zebco 33. It's on a good rod," he said.

We followed the canal into the bay and searched for the reef. I felt the bottom with a stick of 10-foot conduit that he kept in the boat. When he was satisfied we were in the right spot he dropped the anchor.

This time I was ready. I cast first. My cork plunked into the bay and immediately the water churned behind it. I gawked at the phenomenon and popped my cork. The water boiled again. I popped my cork again, and it was … gone.

My drag sizzled and I didn't know what to do. Mr. Raymond sat with his mouth open. Then he came to life. He crawled through the boat and stood beside me peering out at the water as if he could see the fish on my line. He looked at his watch, and then he began coaching me.

Slowly I started horsing the fish in, recapturing some line. Then it made another run and stripped out all my line again. Three times the fish turned and ran, and each time I brought him around.

Mr. Raymond picked up the anchor and let us drift with the fight. My arms ached and burned. Then they quit hurting and became tight and numb. There was nothing to do but stand there and wrestle with whatever swallowed my bait.

Forty minutes from the time I started, Mr. Raymond dip-netted my trophy catch into the boat. It was an African Pompano. The Texas record, that year, was 19 pounds and mine was 17 ½.

Mr. Raymond was happy and had to concede that I'd caught the biggest fish on that trip.

Since then, many experts have said that such a catch on light tackle is impossible. Well, I did it with Mr. Raymond's help. I reckon the echoes of his voice, and those of other old timers that guided me through youth, will always help me conquer the impossible tasks of life.

Learning to Ride – The Hard Way

My best friend, Rusty, bridled and saddled my white mare. It was a nice afternoon, and I was off galavanting while Rusty was running my trapline.

Trapping wasn't too profitable in the early 1970s, but it was an excuse to be in the woods after deer season. It also provided a reason to be horseback. We loved that part of the job. If something couldn't be done horseback it wasn't worth doing. Now, Rusty didn't have much riding experience, but he was full of try.

My white mare was hateful and named after a former Texas Democrat president's wife. Her name was Ladybird. She'd bite, kick, and draw flies all year. Daddy bought her from Lester Dennis in the summer of 1971 and she'd tried to kill me ever since.

Rusty took her through the gate, picked up grandpa's Marlin .22 rifle, and stepped up into the saddle. There was a half-dozen traps set along Yaupon Creek, and another dozen set along Rocky Creek. Then he had to go through the wire-gap at the hay meadow and check sets along the Colorado River. The ride normally took several hours.

Ladybird was a stocky appaloosa without spots. She was sugar-white and a pretty sort of a horse, except for the white around her eyes. She had speed, but sometimes it was hard to control. I used a mechanical hackamore, because the ornery mare would grab the bit in her teeth and turn into the classic "runaway." In short, when the steering failed her brakes quit too.

Rusty knew all her tricks. He rode along Yaupon Creek with the rifle across the saddle in front of him. None of the traps were disturbed. Then he rode across the prairie, started at the west fence, and rode east down Rocky Creek.

The wind had blown the cover off several sets and he stopped to sprinkle leaves and dirt over them. Then he rode to the wire-gap going into the hay bottom. He trotted through the old Johnson grass, to the river, and inspected the sets along its banks. Again, they were undisturbed.

There's nothing like being horseback with a good rifle in your hand and the wind in your face. Rusty didn't care that the traps were empty. The afternoon ride was time well spent. With his chore done he turned the mare for home.

Ladybird's worst trait was being barnsour. Her leisure trot turned into a teeth-jarring, brain-rattling prance. The light touch on the reins turned into a stranglehold-grip to keep her from running.

Rusty dismounted at the wire-gap and led her through. She tried to jerk away and leave him afoot, but he knew that trick and hung onto the reins.

The hard part was remounting with a rifle in one hand. She danced and sidestepped. He finally caught a foot in the stirrup and lunged for the seat – and missed. He landed belly-down across her neck in front of the saddle. This put him in the realms of worst case scenarios. The mare realized her opportunity to pull her runaway trick and bolted into a dead run.

Imagine hanging upside down, with a rifle in one hand, out of control, going full-speed at certain catastrophe. You know this is going to leave a mark.

They tore through the brush along Rocky Creek, crossed the creek, and raced onto the prairie.

Rusty was always extra smart in school and now his high-speed, super sharp, analytical mind that could solve any trigonometry problem turned to survival. He wasn't sure if his guts were going to come out of his ears or his pants legs. It only took him a half-mile of torture to figure out he needed to chunk the rifle. It landed between the horse's feet.

With both hands free, he was in no better shape. He squirmed like a worm on a hook. Then his glasses bounced off. The mare never slacked her Secretariat-jaunt to the feed bucket.

There was only one thing left to do. As the mare skirted another brushline, Rusty made a valiant effort to jump/fall – and landed in a nest of old barbwire.

My Dad was surprised when he answered the doorbell. Rusty was standing there, cut up and bleeding, blind without his glasses, and looking like something the dogs had been playing with.

Together they found his glasses and all the pieces of the rifle. At some point, somebody unsaddled the mare that was waiting at the barn.

Later, Rusty and I decided we needed another horse. I knew where we could buy a two-year-old colt from the Schindler Brother's racing stud, Span Day. He needed a little breaking but I was sure we could do it.

It's a wonder we lived long enough to tell this story. God takes care of the innocent and stupid, or maybe he just likes cowboys.

Establishing Good Habits

We giggled like a couple of little dunces. It was dark and freezing and we were sitting in a tree. Rusty, my running buddy, shivered and blew clouds of steamy breath. Then he poked me, whispered something stupid, and we broke into giggling fits again. We were teenagers, and we were supposed to be deer hunting.

I held his dad's .30-06. It was the first time I'd ever hunted with a scoped rifle.

Dawn began to filter through the darkness. We became quiet and serious. We watched like two stoic little soldiers trying to see deer where there were none. It was unusual not to see any deer.

Then something came out at the corner of the opening. It was over 200 yards away, and was walking away from us at an angle. My mom's antique binoculars fogged up immediately and became useless.

I lifted the rifle and peered through the scope. It took me a while to find the deer, and then I couldn't tell if it had horns.

"Here – you look," I said and handed the rifle to Rusty.

He studied for a good while.

"I can't tell nothing, it's probably a doe," he said.

I took the rifle back and looked again.

"I think it's a buck," I said.

He took the rifle again.

"I can't tell," he said.

Again I took the rifle and my imagination tried to manufacture a rack of horns on the critter's head.

Then the morning sun glinted on an antler. I braced myself to shoot and analyzed where to put the crosshairs. The buck was walking off at a bad angle. I squeezed off.

The recoil surprised me and I lost the sight picture, but Rusty was watching.

"Daddy always says that when a deer runs off you should give him about thirty minutes before you go look for him," Rusty said. So, we waited five minutes and went to look.

There was no blood – just what we thought could have been a couple of pieces of hair.

There was a light frost in the opening, but under the brush the leaves were damp and quiet. We followed what we thought was his tracks to the creek, and worried that we were on the wrong trail. We marked the spot where we started.

On the other side of the creek we found blood; or rather Rusty found blood. For a short distance, Rusty walked along pointing at the ground. I followed along trying to see what he was pointing at. The trail led us further into the brush, and then it petered out.

We marked our last spot and searched on our hands and knees, careful not to crawl over any fresh sign. Then Rusty picked up the trail again.

The next three hours were an agonizing learning experience. The deer didn't leave much sign, and we discussed the consequences of taking a bad shot. I was feeling bad.

Rusty was doing the majority of the finding. We would lose the trail and then he'd find it again. Sometimes we positioned ourselves where the deer was standing, and guessed where to look next.

The deer was traveling up a long gradual hill, and that didn't seem right. Ciphering his trail was slow. There was barely enough blood to tease us on, but as long as we kept finding tiny pinhead-size drops we continued. I was disgusted.

We had taken eye tests at school. The nurse had declared me color blind, but I hadn't believed the old gal.

Now I was finding the full effect of the annoying handicap. I could see the blood once Rusty showed it to me, but it was seldom that I found it first. The best thing to do was to touch it with my finger, and then look at my finger. For some reason I could see the red color on my hand better than on the ground.

I was exasperated, but as long as there was the slightest clue we stayed with our chore.

Rusty crawled taking a near-sighted perspective of the situation. I walked hunched over taking careful steps well to the side of where the trail should be. We were nearly a half-mile from where we had started.

Then maybe we heard something, or maybe a movement alerted us but we looked ahead and saw the buck lying in a tiny opening. He was dying; and by the time we got to him it was over.

Rusty and I were in our formative years. We learned a little about tracking deer, but we learned more about ourselves.

Sometimes I find myself on a dim trail. Sometimes I'm blind to any sign that would show me how to continue. Quitting is never an option. Perseverance is its own reward.

Hunter Ethics and Lying

- Texas, 1979

Frivolous thoughts frittered through our minds at light speed. Structured ideas had little chance to root themselves into our thinking. Incessant grins creased our smooth faces. Fresh air gave us Herculean abilities. We were slim, hard, strong, and young – and God loved us.

The outfitter eyeballed me. He saw an easy mark.
"Now, for three hundred and fifty dollars you can spend a day and shoot a world class Texas Dall sheep," he said.

I nodded and averted my eyes from meeting his, looking down and flipping through the pages of his photo album. I only cared about hunting white-tails. The sudden influx of exotics into the area didn't interest me, and his hunts didn't sound any harder than shooting your neighbor's milk cow.

Then he figured me out.

"Look, I know a man who bought a bunch of mouflon ewes. The rams he bought were Corsicans. He wants to get rid of those rams and raise purebred mouflons. You can shoot a Corsican ram for eighty-five dollars."

"If you bring a buddy along, you can each shoot a ram for seventy-five dollars. And I think I can swing it so if you bring two buddies you can shoot three rams for sixty-five dollars apiece. You'd be doing this guy a favor and getting a nice trophy for yourself."

The outfitter didn't know it but he had me hooked.

"Where is the ranch?" I asked. "Is this behind a high fence?"

"The ranch is in Schulenburg and it's open range. The sheep are running free," he said. We parted and I agreed to call him back. Then I hurried home to confer with my accomplices, Rusty and Hoelscher.

One week later, the outfitter met us in Schulenburg and led us to the ranch. At first glance, there was nothing fancy about it. There was no great entrance, no paved drives, nothing to indicate a wealthy exotic big game breeder lived here. There was only an aluminum gate and a pasture road that passed a renovated farmhouse. The place didn't appear any different than a hundred other German or Bohemian farms in the area. The only standout feature was a single engine airplane under a shed.

"How big is this place?" I asked.

Rusty and Hoelscher's heads cranked around on their skinny little necks and they gawked at the outfitter.

"It's about eighty acres," he said.

Rusty and Hoelscher looked big-eyed at me and I looked back at them. Then we all focused on the outfitter.

"If these sheep are wild, what keeps them from leaving?" I asked.

"Well, we've got permission to go on the neighbor's if we have to. Get in the back of the truck and we'll see if we can find them."

We did as we were told and spent the next 30 minutes bouncing around the countryside trying to make a road kill. Then one of the Mexican workers stopped us and told our guide the sheep were grazing on an oats patch behind the farmhouse.

Rusty and Hoelscher woofed at me.

"Yeah, these sheep are wild," Rusty said. "Shake a coffee can of corn and they come running."

Hoelscher was laughing, "Herman, please don't shoot that ram while his head is in the bucket."

I held out hopes that it wasn't going to be that easy – and it wasn't. The pickup eased to a stop and the sheep stampeded into the brush. It seemed obvious they knew the difference between a rifle and a corn bucket.

The rest of the morning was spent spotting and stalking. Hoelscher made an excellent long range shot, while I made a close sneak for a try with my Winchester. Rusty closed out the action with three valiant running shots. The first two were clean misses and probably killed somebody in China, but his last poke was true.

Our guide was noticeably absent for much of the hunt and when the smoke cleared he showed up with another hunter. The guy was short, round, blonde, and resembled the Pillsbury Doughboy.

"Hey guys, would y'all help me get this man a fallow deer? Then we can field dress everything at once." he said.

We nodded and loaded up in the pickup again, us in the back. We didn't have a clue what was about to happen, but we all studied the guy's stainless steel rifle case. None of us had ever seen anything like it.

The truck stopped at a high fence we didn't know existed. On the other side of the wire were two fallow bucks and a white-tailed buck. They grazed and looked at us. The hunter let the tailgate down and opened his rifle case. We stood back admiring his rifle. Then he walked over to the fence, knelt on one knee, stuck his rifle through a wire square, and blasted one of the fallow bucks. You could have knocked us over with a feather, we were horrified.

After that, conversation became sparse. We didn't know how to talk to these people. They were too different from us. We did our duty and field dressed the fallow buck. Then took a few pictures with our rams and quartered them. By mid-afternoon we were ready to head home, but before we left I took a picture of the airplane.

"You know, we're not going to tell people we shot these sheep in Schulenburg," I said. Rusty and Hoelscher started to grin. "We just got back from a hunt in Las Vegas, New Mexico, on a ranch so big the landowner needed an airplane to look at all of it."

By the time we hit the county line the story was in full bloom.

Who Shot C.R.?

The boys took turns cornering me. As deer season neared, they came by the house individually to interrogate me.

"Hey, Herman... what's going to be the rules for shooting a buck this year?" they asked.

The previous year, I convinced everyone to let all the bucks walk. We practiced restraint trying to manage our deer, but we didn't have the scientific information to know what we were doing.

Now, there was evidence we'd been doing it wrong. Texas Parks and Wildlife was kicking around a 13-inch inside spread antler regulation and it looked like a good deal.

I was in a dilemma. My feelings were that we needed to continue letting the bucks walk, but I knew my friends were anxious to do some trophy hunting. The situation had me grinding my teeth and pulling my hair.

Shaws Bend has become so fragmented among countless landowners it's hard to sit in a deer stand and not watch some other yahoo sitting in a deer stand across the fence. I have a hard time perceiving this as a form of hunting.

Then a good thing happened, but it didn't stop me from worrying. Jerold Wayne Koehl headed up a push to start a wildlife cooperative and most of the landowners jumped on board. We did some spotlight surveys to count the deer, and I saw just how fragmented the area had become. There were a lot of deer in cornfields at one end of Shaws Bend. But, there were equal numbers in peoples' yards, under nightlights and nibbling in flowerbeds, at the other end. The whole thing seemed like a big neighborhood with a bunch of pet deer running around.

So, with the wildlife co-op in place and the TPW scientific management tools under our belt, I compromised my thoughts and answered my friends.

"Okay boys, let's start the thirteen-inch rule a year early. If y'all see something with a thirteen-inch inside spread – go ahead," I said.

We had several more discussions and assured ourselves we all knew how to recognize a mature buck. I crossed my fingers, held my breath, and hoped there wouldn't be any mistakes. It seemed like a good test.

Sure enough…

The first morning of the season one of the boys came to the house.

"Herman, come help me pick up this buck I shot. I know he's big enough, nobody would pass up a deer like this," he said.

We crawled in the truck and headed through the pasture to his stand. The deer was laying within 100 yards of his stand in a big opening. I pulled up alongside the expired critter and looked out the window.

"It's thirteen inches, don't you think?" he asked.

"Nope, that's a 12–inch spread on a two-and-a-half-year-old deer. He's an eight-pointer that was trying to make nine. He's exactly the kind of animal we want to let walk. But... he's dead now, let's load him," I said.

The rest of the ride was awkward. My buddy kept saying he couldn't see anyone letting a good buck like that go by, but I reiterated if we want to have mature bucks we have to have mercy on the young ones. A good hunter knows restraint. It was a good thing the 13-inch rule wasn't legally coming into effect until next year – lesson learned.

A few days later I called him on the phone.

"Hey man, you know the neighbor-lady that lives over here in Alfred Schobel's old house?" I asked.

"Yeah," he said.

"Well, it seems she had a buck that slept in her yard every night under the nightlight. Every morning before she went to work, she fed him a couple of cinnamon rolls. She even called him C. R. He liked to play with her cats, and she had to watch he didn't hook the wash off her clothesline. She's been feeding him all summer. Now, she called me bawling and squalling because she hasn't seen him since the first day of deer season," I said.

"Nooooo," he said.

"Yep... man, you shot C.R.," I said.

There was a long silence on the other end of the phone.

This year the 13-inch rule will be legally in effect for the second year. I've seen a pile of two-and-a-half-year-old eight-pointers. There are also a few that are better than eight and will be hard to judge. I'm telling my hunters that before they pull the trigger, they better be ready to take their prize to the voluntary check station.

Grandpa's Gun

Harvey Poenitzsch and I were going to haul hay. Spring was becoming serious summertime, and we had the windows rolled down on the International pickup truck.

"I'm giving you a raise," Harvey said. He didn't smile when he said it, but he doesn't smile much or waste many words either.

"How much you going to pay me?" I asked.

"I'll start paying you two-and-a-half cents a bale."

I sat there and tried to not let my face change as I wondered what rate he used to cipher my wages before the raise. Up to that point, Harvey paid me whenever he figured I'd earned about $50.

I was a runt when I was a junior in high school and maybe I wasn't worth much, but I tried hard. Working for Harvey was the first and last purely honest job I've ever had. It was one of the last summers of childhood and was one of the finer experiences that I've carried with me through life.

When I wasn't hauling hay, Rusty my running partner and I were tearing down an old barn and using the boards to build a new deer stand. It was a mansion. It was a tower with six-foot legs and was big enough for two people. It had glass windows that could be put up or down and a swivel stool from Aunt Verlie Brune's cafe (the cafe was where Prause's hospital supply is now). It even had a remnant of carpet on the floor. There was tarpaper on the roof and I planned on doing some intense buck hunting in that stand.

The most essential tool for the coming hunting season would come from the hay-hauling money. I wanted a new rifle. Grandpa's 1873 Winchester.44-40 wasn't adequate anymore. The old gun just didn't have the range I needed. I'd killed several deer with it, but I wanted a real deer rifle that could reach out and touch something.

I saved my money and in August went to visit Raymond Untemeyer. He was a gunsmith, and the best gun expert I knew. Plus, Mr. Raymond didn't mind talking guns to a kid. His small shop was a cozy haven full of Remington and Winchester treasures.

We discussed calibers and decided that a .30-06 was the right size for me. Then we talked about gun makers. I leaned towards Winchester, but he had no problem with Remington and said that I'd be doing all right to buy either type. The price of such a rifle was about $185.

Then he told me to wait. He started digging under his workbench and momentarily came out with a new rifle. I'd never seen such a rifle. He began showing me why it was better than other guns that I'd looked at, and he made an easy sale. In minutes I was $245 lighter and was the happiest kid on the block. I walked out of his shop not knowing that the Sako rifle I purchased was one of the few good investments I would ever make.

The opening day of deer season meant more to Rusty and I than Christmas. When summer was over we agonized through several months suffocating within the impregnable brick-walled, airtight school buildings. During our suffering we half-heartedly listened to the mutterings of our poor dejected teachers. Their lectures sounded like muffled, distant echoes reverberating from the inside of an ignored barrel; or like a scratchy-sounding radio that's losing reception and that nobody is listening to. Our minds and souls lived in the open fresh air of the live oak woods and the yaupon brush - and our grades showed it.

When deer season finally came I was in my new deer stand at five a.m. I sat there most of the first day watching crows and squirrels eat corn at my feeder. I was there again the next day and every afternoon after school for the next week. I sat in my new deer stand knowing that ol' mossyhorn was going to step out any minute. It was a great aggravation knowing that he probably came by while I was wasting my days in school.

The days turned into weeks and there was no indication that the hunting was going to improve. Time began to drag and my spirits began to sag. The long hours sitting in the deer stand began to seem pointless. Several weeks passed and the critters with antlers were not making themselves available to my new hunting technology.

On Thanksgiving morning it was threatening rain. A front was coming in soon. I put the new rifle in the corner and got grandpa's gun out of the closet. I wrapped it with a plastic bag from the dry cleaners and walked out of the house. Instead of going to the new deer stand, I went down into the brush and sat beside a log on a gravel bar in Rocky Creek.

I unwrapped the old '73 Winchester and waited. At daylight a feral housecat crossed the creek and spent a long time studying me while I sat stone still. Then a doe came from the brush and tiptoed through the leaves along the opposite creek bank. My nerves began to tingle as I heard something following her. Then I saw him.

I thumbed the hammer back and raised the rifle in one motion. It tucked naturally against me and I aimed the familiar iron sights behind the buck's shoulder. Without the benefits of glass windows, a swivel stool, or a cornfeeder, and without the help of a high-powered, scoped rifle, I collected my first eight-pointer.

I never knew my grandfather who owned the gun. He died three years before I was born. But that cool drizzly Thanksgiving morning down in the yaupon brush along Rocky Creek, I didn't feel alone when I got up to go look at the deer.

It's usually not the rifle that's inadequate – it's the man behind it.

Following the Hounds to see Old Tracks

D emon, Donnie, Junior, and Willie were in the brush ahead of me. They were a long way ahead of me. I sloshed through ankle deep water. The yaupon and tangle briars snagged my clothes and tripped me. Then I stopped and listened for the hounds.

The early dawn cold had turned into a sweaty muggy morning. I was panting under layers of clothes. Spring rains were flooding the country. All the creeks were running bank-full and the prairies were knee-deep muck.

It was perfect for hog hunting.

I traveled as fast as I could, following the dogs, but my going was slow. Somewhere behind me, Crockett was following on his ATV four-wheeler.

The air was thick enough to chew. I stopped beneath the canopy of yaupon to catch my breath and loosen my jackets. I stood there inspecting the confines of the tight, dripping woods and drifted into a daydream.

Grandpa Brune died in 1954, and I never knew him. But I grew up listening to hunting stories about him, and I live in a house that has 25 of his mounted deer heads. A picture of grandpa with his rifle and an eight-point buck hangs in the hall.

Uncle Munroe told me they chased a coon around the Hillcrest Dance Hall three times while a band was playing inside. All the folks in the hall quit dancing and came out to listen to the music of the hounds.

My neighbor lady, Mrs. Willie Mae Smahlik, says she was a little girl on the way to church with her parents, and met grandpa on the road. He was horseback and was headed home after a night of hunting.

I envisioned Mrs. Willie's expression while she related the meeting. There was no doubt, the sight of the man on horseback with his hounds trailing along made an impression.

The stories are bittersweet to me. I enjoy hearing them, but they also make me sad. I missed something. I missed knowing him. I missed a place in time when the quality of life was infinitely simpler.

Then a distant, muffled yelp pierced through my daze and brought me back to reality. I'd been standing there with my mouth hanging half-open and my eyes beginning to glaze – asleep on my feet.

Now, I listened. It was Demon's hoarse, coughing bay that brought me back to life. I took off again slugging my way through the brush and mire.

Demon never barks on the trail. He never chases deer, and he doesn't bother cattle. He's old – probably a bit senile – and loves to bite pigs. He is 90 percent foolproof. He won't make a sound unless he's got a hog in sight, or the scent is burning fresh. The only thing he'll occasionally do wrong is tree a coon.

It was curious, Demon was the only dog I could hear. However, it was possible they had struck a sow with pigs and the other dogs were chasing scattered piglets. There was no way to guess; the only thing to do was fight through the tangle and get to him.

I'd never been in this nest before. I wasn't lost, but I didn't see anything familiar. The head of Dry Branch Creek was somewhere around here.

Then I heard Demon again. He was near.

I eased along. My eyes getting wider as I approached and spotted the dog. My nerves began to jump as I looked for the wild pig. Demon trotted in a circle, baying in his raspy old voice, and then disappeared behind a giant post oak tree.

I was wringing wet with sweat, it poured off me like I'd stuck my head in a bucket.

Ten yards from the tree, I pulled my pistol.

The thought of the work – dragging a stinking black monster boar hog from the bowels of these steaming brushy woods didn't bother me. That's what we had come to do; and we'd abstain from shooting before we'd leave meat lying on the ground.

The tree was so big that I had to make a wide loop to see behind it.

There was Demon. He had his front feet against the post oak and his muzzle pointed towards the sky. I holstered my gun. The old rascal had bayed-up a coon.

Then I looked closer at the tree.

Crockett showed up lanking and ducking his long frame through the low-hanging brush.

"What's he got Brune?" Crockett asked.

"A coon," I said.

Crockett muttered some hateful words in the dog's direction.

"But look what else I found," I said.

Post oaks are often hollow. Long years ago a coon had climbed this tree to escape the hounds. It had gone into a hole about 12 feet from the ground. The hunters, suspecting the hollow extended to the base of the tree, chopped into it. They were right, and opened a good-size hole in the side of the oak. Then they cut a length of green wispy yaupon and stuck it in the hole trying to poke the coon and make him go out the top. The yaupon stick was still in the hollow tree, but it had turned too brittle to extract.

Nobody knows if the plan worked. The axe marks on the post oak tree were ancient. As Crockett led his dog away, I put my hand on the rough bark and looked up at the tree's branches.

I thought about grandpa Brune, I tried to hear the echo of hounds from long ago, and I wondered if I was standing in grandpa's tracks.

Grandma Made Me Proud
of Who I Am

She sat on the screened-in back porch on a hard wooden chair. Her hands were folded in her lap and tucked into a pair of cotton jersey gloves. Her skirt was long, thin, and almost colorless from wear. A scarf protected her head. An old patched over-sized jacket cloaked her top half.

She was a small thin woman. The years bent her frame; she hunched forward at the shoulders. Her generation had seen America go from the horse and buggy to the fast impersonal age of the auto and high-tech industry. She was old and often seemed tired, but her eyes and mind remained sharp and clear. She had a lifetime of family memories, and she always had a laugh and a happy story to tell.

I drove up and parked between the house and the barn. The young woman with me stepped out of the passenger side of the truck and hauled out grandpa's old Winchester. I reached into the vehicle, brought out my .30-06, and together we started to walk down the backside of the hill.

Grandma's call stopped us.

"Hi, Herman Willie."

I looked to the house on the hill and waved to the small figure on the porch.

"Hi, grandma," I said.

"Hi, grandma," the gal with me said.

We continued around the barn, down the hill, and past the windmill. A few steps farther we came to a pecan tree. I held the rifles as the young woman climbed the steps nailed to the side of the tree. Ten feet from the ground were two boards fastened across a couple of limbs for a seat. She made herself comfortable and I started up the tree. She reached down to take the old gun from me, and I picked my way through the branches until I was wedged onto the seat beside her. She jacked a cartridge into the chamber and eased the hammer into the safety position. We were ready. My female partner had never hunted deer before.

A few does with a forked-horn yearling came out and nibbled the oats at the edge of the patch. Then a six-pointer charged onto the scene. He dogged a circle around the rest of the deer and then trotted along a fence line paralleling the creek at the bottom of the hill.

"Do you have a shot?" I asked.

"I can't see him."

"What do you mean? He's right there!"

She wiped her eye, and I could tell that she was straining to see across the iron sights.

"I don't have a shot," she said.

"Okay, just wait he's gone now, maybe he'll come back."

I watched the buck as he veered from the fence line, entered the brush along the creek, and then started to sneak back to the does.

"What about that one?" she asked. She was looking at the does while I watched the six-pointer.

"That's a fork-horn," I said.

"No, that one," she said.

I swiveled to see what she was blabbering about and my mouth fell open. BULLWINKLE had stepped out of the brush.

"Shoot that…"

BLAM! My statement was cut short by the blast of the Winchester. The buck bit the dirt like he'd been hit by a train, but he didn't stay down. It was a spine shot. Death was imminent if not graceful.

My heart rate was going off the charts. The buck was trying to crawl off and I thought my hunter was shaking too bad to make another shot. I didn't know the right thing to do, so I raised my .30-06 and finished the commotion.

"You got him honey he's yours. Let's go look at him," I said.

We slid out of the tree like a couple of squirrels and long-walked toward the girl's first trophy.

A loud whoop surprised us. Grandma was hurrying down the hill. She was using her walking cane and a pair of antique binoculars dangled from her neck.

"I watched the whole thing," grandma said. "I could see y'all and the deer from the back porch. C'mon let's look at him. I think he's a big one." She was tickled to be in on the hunt, and we were tickled to have her join the party.

This little event happened a lifetime ago. It was when fall days were cold and sharing them with a young wife and a grandmother made a 21-year-old man feel happy, grown, and complete.

Grandma Brune passed away in 1983. But every time I drive up to grandma's house I look at the back porch. I know she's there. I'm glad she's watching.

~MEXICO~

Good Attitude, the First Ingredient for Success

Howard shook my hand and smiled. His manners and easy demeanor made me feel good. He was excited and looking forward to his hunt. Hopefully, his great disposition would help us deal with the tough hunting we faced.

Howard watched too many hunting shows on television and fell prey to the same outfitter who shanghaied me to guide whitetail hunters in Mexico. The 140,000-acre ranch was divided amongst six guides. My area was about 30,000 acres and had two deer stands. However, after several days of scouting I decided the only critters visiting those stands were javelina.

Howard also expected to see an assortment of muy grande bucks. He paid $4,850 to hunt four days, sleep and eat at the cushy hacienda, and be guided by a whitetail expert. I had bad news for him. The Mexican desert was saturated with mountain lions. The only grande bucks we'd found were the lion kills. But I had a plan, and Howard seemed happy and ready to go. He had a genuine good soul.

The first morning we left camp in the dark. I parked the truck in a shallow brushy wash at the base of a ridge. Then I whispered to Howard.

"It's an easy hike up this ridge. We're going to follow it a few hundred yards and come out above a water hole. There's lots of deer sign here, and I put corn out yesterday. I'll bring along some folding stools and we'll sit in the brush and wait," I said.

Howard nodded his approval.

"Just go slow," he said.

We picked our way through the cactus, and he scared me when he stumbled and piled up in the first 50 yards. But, he got up and was game to keep going. The rest of the hike went without incident and we found a good spot to wait.

It was a great morning. The gradual dawn coaxed the Mexican desert to life. The waterhole's smooth glassy surface was speckled with ducks. Songbirds worked through the brush, and a Mexican Golden Eagle hung like a kite in the pale sky. Deer appeared immediately. A couple of young bucks found the corn but didn't spend much time eating. They seemed to be traveling. We glassed and followed their movements. Then we held our position until long after the show was over.

The exhibition of wildlife warranted further observation. We sat on the ridge again that evening and again the next morning, but each time we saw fewer deer. I noted the hike and lack of results were wearing on Howard. He didn't complain, but I figured I needed a new plan.

The second evening we tried one of the stands and had one good size buck blitz by us. The third morning we returned to the stand and saw nothing.

I became irritated, but I knew the deer were beginning to rut. I began searching out every nook and fold in the hills, looking for a chance to rattle in a good buck –no cigar. Howard marveled at some of the little guys that came running, but no big buster bucks appeared.

I started covering a lot of ground.

Howard enjoyed the truck-riding time. The desert and the critters intrigued him. He asked question after question, and I surprised myself by having most of the answers. His desire for knowledge pleased me. He enjoyed the fresh air and breadth of the ranch. He was amazed at the quantity of life that the barren country produced. His enthusiasm was infectious. His joy was pure. He was happy just to be there. He made me feel he was happy to be with me.

The last morning was spent driving and glassing. I stopped to open a gate and spotted a lone doe on a near hillside.

"Howard, get out of the truck and get ready. Let's see what comes out of the brush below that doe," I said.

He moved forward and rested his rifle over the gatepost.

The 10-pointer, he took, was the biggest trophy in camp. It was also the biggest buck he'd ever gotten.

Howard's spirit and attitude turned a tough hunt into a fun week, and I felt like I'd made a new friend. He booked to hunt with us again the next year.

Cats That Don't Like Petting

The hunters bellied up to a round table in the hacienda's dining room. It was suppertime. Mexican waiters served drinks and kept the food coming as the men ate and gabbed about nothing of consequence. They were a bunch of middle aged rich guys enjoying a cush deer hunt on a 140,000-acre Mexico ranch.

The outfitter made himself right at home between the hunters being waited on hand and foot while laughing a little too loud at stories that weren't funny.

The landowner patrolled between the kitchen and the eaters assuring they were satiated. He was a younger man, tall, stately, educated in Monterrey, and probably a social class above his guests.

I sat at a different table with the other guides, half-listening to their conversation and watching the rest of the room. Then the landowner gave a subtle nod to one of his hired men and eased out the door. No one else noticed his departure.

Earlier, the head guide found a dead yearling colt – killed by a mountain lion. Throughout the previous weeks we'd discovered four big bucks and one doe killed in similar fashion. It seems the older bucks that travel alone are easier prey.

Everyone in camp knew the rancher was going spotlighting for the killer cat. Some of the gringo hunters asked to go along, but he'd smiled and avoided giving an answer. He preferred to take a couple of his cowboys.

The waiters began clearing the plates and I retired to the pool table where I lost the first game. The room felt stuffy and I headed for the hacienda's yard and some fresh air. The clients and one of the other guides followed me.

The evening was cool and bullbats dove at bugs attracted to the outside lights. Stars were coming out and I stood peering into the evening sky breathing in the openness of the desert and looking stupidly at constellations I didn't know.

Then the cattle guard rattled and the rancher's truck chugged into the yard. He was riding in the highrack and one his cowboys was driving. They backed up to the skinning shed.

I was surprised at his quick return and called up to him.

"You already get something?"

"Yep, he was feeding on the horse."

I hurried to gawk at the horse-killer and the man gave me a strange warning.

"Be careful, he may not be dead!"

I smirked at the idea of loading a live mountain lion in the back of a truck and never hesitated – but the critter wasn't lying against the tailgate where I'd expected. It was lying on its side, draped over a spare tire, stretched out with its feet against the cab. Its head was on the driver side and its tail extended down the truck bed on the passenger side.

My excitement overcame good sense as I moved around the vehicle and reached through the angle iron braces of the highrack.

The instant my hand touched the tan hide I saw the cat's ribs heave with a labored breath. I jerked my arm away as the cat sat up, bared its teeth inches from my face, and pierced the night's serenity with a bloodcurdling snarl.

I don't remember moving but in the blink of an eye I was twenty feet away. Doors slammed behind me as the hunters and other guide jumped into a Suburban. I was set to run but something stopped me. I stood, amazed, staring and studying. The feline's eyes couldn't focus and he wasn't moving his feet. All he could do was sit there and growl.

Out of the corner of my eye I saw an old Mexican cowboy. He was carrying a lariat and building a loop. He meant to get the rope on the cat, take a wrap on a post under the shed, and let the driver pull ahead. I grinned and moved to help.

We started fishing the lasso through the angle iron but it was difficult to hold your ground every time the kitty snarled, and we were having problems keeping the loop open.

Then the other guide yelled at me as he crept out of the Suburban.

"Y'all are crazy, get away from that thing, he's going to bite you!"

"No he ain't," I said. I couldn't look away and explain why it wasn't going to bite me, but I knew it couldn't.

The other guide continued to rail at me.

"Get away from that thing, I'm going to shoot it."

"What kind of gun do you have?" I asked.

"A seven MM magnum!"

"You can't shoot that cannon into the back of this man's truck."

Finally, the rancher spoke up.

"I'll shoot him boys, I've got a twenty-two and it won't hurt anything," he said.

He pointed the small rifle one-handed and ended the episode.

We dropped the tailgate and slid the lion out onto the ground. With all my years of guiding, this was the first wild mountain lion I'd ever seen. And I could honestly say that I petted it before it met it's demise.

Next time I'll listen when someone warns me about double checking dangerous game that is supposed to be dead.

Trust Your Friends and Keep One Hand on Your Pocketbook

now pellets stung my face and gale winds bulleted the white ice through the air. I stood on a high ridge with my back hunched into the wind and my head pulled deep into the collar of my big coats. The Mexican desert looked empty.

The hunter I guided stood behind me bracing against the wind, but seemed otherwise unconcerned. He was a television preacher from West Texas and his congregation anted $4,850 for his four-day white-tailed deer hunt in Mexico. I needed to change professions.

I turned to talk to him and pulled my face farther into my coats, squinting my eyes to avoid the piercing frozen crystals.

"Here I am in sunny Old Mexico, standing on a ridge, watching the snow blow sideways," I said. "One of us ain't been living right!

I don't know what you've been doing but I've been behaving myself!"

My hunter grinned and nodded. We walked off the ridge to find a better vantage point that would give us a look into the protected nooks and crannies in the valley. I already knew what we were going to find – nothing.

It was the fourth and final hunt on the 140,000-acre ranch. The first three hunts were disappointments and I didn't have any false hopes about old muy grande popping out of the woodwork. The only big bucks we'd found were mountain lion kills. Each guide had 30,000 acres to hunt and we were steadily trespassing on each other hoping to find something someone else missed. I knew how many does and young bucks lived in each valley of my area. But it was my job to guide and keep hunting, so I did.

There were six hunters in camp and six conscientious guides who continuously scoured the country. The outfitter never showed up, and every night the conversation around the supper table was a little quieter and a little less cordial. Everyday the guides searched harder hoping for a miracle.

The television preacher was a good man, a good walker, and a good hunter. We spent quality time visiting and getting to know each other. But finally, on the last day he vented his frustrations.

"What's going on Herman?" he asked. "This hunt was a gift from my congregation. It's not going anything like I expected, and from what I understand y'all haven't done well on the other hunts. I could understand if it was just tough going, but the deer aren't here. We were sold on the idea there were plenty of trophy bucks. How can an outfitter sell such an expensive hunt on a ranch that doesn't have any deer?"

I was quiet for a minute. I wanted to pick my words and give an honest answer.

"Well for one thing, this is the first year that we've been on this ranch," I said. "Last year the outfitter came down here and hunted for two days. The landowner guided him and, of course, knew where to take him. In those two days he saw four one-forty plus Boone & Crockett class bucks and shot a one-fifty-eight. He thought the whole ranch was covered with deer like that and he leased the place. Now, what we've found is the place is crawling with mountain lions. It's also been a dry year. Deer don't grow good antlers in dry years. I've hunted four other ranches this year and antler size is down all over the country. The bottom line is the outfitter believed there were a lot more deer and a lot more good bucks."

The preacher thought about what I said, but my words weren't strong enough to heal his dissatisfaction. Late in the day we separated to glass different directions and he shot a small buck. He went home with mixed feelings about his experience.

It was time for me to have a serious talk with myself. I wanted to quit guiding. In 12 years I worked for three different outfitters in Montana and two different outfitters in Texas and Mexico. I knew all the standard excuses for having a bad hunt. I knew all the standard excuses for having less than adequate camps. I knew all the standard excuses an outfitter could use. I was tired of making new friends only to see them go home unhappy.

Then the word came from my current boss. He was leasing the ranch for another year. His reputation was built from being associated with a big-time outdoor product manufacturer and he had hunters lined up. He wanted to make hay while the sun was shining.

That was it! I quit! I might miss the camps and meeting new people, but I wouldn't miss seeing them hurt. After 12 years of guiding I was going home to Shaws Bend and hanging it up.

A few months later a call came from one of the boys I'd guided with. He was starting his own business. He had a primo 30,000-acre open range ranch leased in Mexico and wanted me. Then a call came from Wyoming. Another wilderness outfitter wanted me, and he came with strong references from a man I'd previously guided.

In 2002 I lived in two of the best camps imaginable. The one in Mexico had abundant trophy bucks and a five-star lodge. The one in Wyoming was everything a high country camp and elk hunt is supposed to be.

Moral #1: Never stop believing in yourself, your standards, or the things you love.

Moral #2: Picking an outfitter is harder than picking your kinfolks. Word-of-mouth is always the best reference.

Guiding the Rich
and Famous

"**D**on't let that man shoot anything less than a hundred-fifty class buck!" He stared me down. It was a rare serious moment, but the remark seemed moot. At $6,000 a whack, nobody wants less. The hunter I was to guide is a television personality – on a channel I don't watch, with a TV hunting show I've never seen. His program has aired 17 years, but I quit watching the boob tube in 1980.

However, I was not oblivious. I'd heard of his company and the toys and videos they sold. The fact his business is prospering is proof enough I'm out of touch with society, or at least the pay-to-shoot genre of hunters.

But, that conclusion seems condemning. His company also provides a service to outdoorsman and conservation, while raising money for homeless and hungry in his home state. To heck with me if it's not my style.

The guy is a nice man and would be a good neighbor. It would be like living next door to any charity-driven retired professional athlete whose hair never gets mussed.

His hectic schedule allowed him to hunt only four days, and the first day went great. We didn't see any deer for me to judge. There was the usual troupe of two, and three-year-old bucks with a few does. But we were looking for five-and-a-half-year-old trophies.

The second day was different and I got a whiff of trouble to come. For starters, we were hunting safari style. In Africa, hunters drive until game is spotted or sign is found. Then a stalk is made from the vehicle. In Texas, or Mexico, they just shoot from the back of the truck – a disgusting habit to us wilderness guides.

We were puttering along when a dark-bodied buck stepped into the middle of the road. I stopped and jumped up into the highrack.

"What do you think?" the hunter asked.

The camera man gave me a sideways glance and looked back into his eyepiece.

"Well sir, that's a real nice eight-pointer," I said, and I peered through my binoculars. "He might go one-forty, but I tell you what – I think he's only four-and-a-half-years-old. Aren't you looking for something bigger? This is only the second day. We need something older and bigger. Let's wait."

The camera man spewed a sigh of relief and the hunter ignored him. I looked from one to the other and moved back down into the cab.

The scene confused me and later I queried the cameraman.

"What's the deal?" I asked. "He was ready to blast a cull buck."

"Aw, he just wants to get it over with," the cameraman said. "We don't want him shooting anything too little. This is for television. He needs to shoot a big trophy or go without."

I studied the cameraman for a second, not agreeing or disagreeing. There were doubts backlogging in my mind.

The third day I learned my hunter would leave at 10:00 a.m. the next morning. The entire day was filled with comments like "if I see eight points I'm dropping the hammer." I was becoming more confounded about my duty, but also convinced that the TV personality was a regular Joe.

The fourth morning I put the video duo in a tower stand. Then I crawled up on a windmill and froze. Dawn simmered into daylight and the Mexican wildlife trotted to life with the sun. Deer were everywhere. I counted seven bucks. One of them was a mature eight-pointer – another management buck. I watched him and noted the trail he was traveling. When I left my perch I drove in the opposite direction.

We skirted the perimeter of the ranch and I was about to put out the fire and call the dogs when ol' Mr. Rich and Famous stopped me.

"Herman, look at this buck!"

I leaped into the highrack.

"Yes sir, what you got?" I examined our prey in my long glasses.

"Is that a mature buck?" he asked.

"Well, he's as good an eight-pointer as we've seen. But if you need a ten-point for TV we better wait."

The buck was tending a doe and moved a short distance through the brush. I hopped down to counter its movement with the truck, then climbed back into the highrack. Meanwhile, a discussion erupted between the two filmmakers.

"Herman, is that a mature buck?" again came the question. The man was cranked down behind his riflescope.

"Yes sir, that's a mature buck."

This time my answer was a shot and the show was over.

The next hour was consternating. The cameraman was beside himself. The outfitter was perplexed, and my shooter gathered his duffel. Then he called me aside.

"Herman, you did a good job," he said. Then he shook my hand and handed me a generous tip.

I nodded and satisfied myself with the thought I had a happy hunter. I'd done my duty.

~ M O N T A N A ~

Valentines is a Special Day, Like Everyday

C old rain blew in my face while I packed the mules for the summer trip. The nerves in my temples twitched and I ground my teeth, there was a high pitched whining in my ears. I was anxious, agitated, and a little scared.

Then I looked up at the little girl child sitting on the big black horse. My jaw dropped and my heart sank. She was so small. She was bundled in several layers of clothing topped by a green florescent rain jacket with a hood over her wool cap. Her hands were tucked into mittens and held the reins. Only her tiny clear face was exposed and it was screwed into a grimace. She was trying not to cry – my daughter so little and so scared.

Her mother took her and moved away when she was three, now she was six. My lone cowboy lifestyle and my ignorance of the courts cost me too much. A big piece of my life was missing. This was my first chance to be with her for a normal summer visit, and we were headed into the wilderness for an eight-day pack trip.

I left the mule I was loading and went to her. Patting her on the leg I gazed into her eyes and assured her.

"It's going to be okay Sam," I said. "This ol' pony's name is Lunar and he's going to take care of you. He knows where we're going and he'll follow the cook to camp. I'll be there when you get there."

Some of the tension left her. I saw she felt better knowing she could trust the horse and knowing she wouldn't be alone on the journey. Maybe she felt better knowing I wasn't leaving her.

The trail wound up and over the high magnificent Headquarters Pass. Most of the mountains were still snow-capped and we criss-crossed an icy trickling stream. It spread in sparkling tendrils across the bare granite, then splashed down the mountain to become the Teton River. At mid-day the sun broke out and my mood warmed.

There were eight guests and three work hands on the camping trip. At noon the pilgrims stopped in a lush alpine basin for lunch while the mule strings continued to their destination. The air was crisp and clean and had the effect of cleansing a person's worries away. I glimpsed my daughter smiling and enjoying the company, the ride, and the day.

She was an automatic hit in camp. She flitted amongst the guests and caught frogs in the creek, naming one of them and catching it again and again on a daily schedule. Whenever the cook called she ran to the wall tent to help with chores, too small to do anything with heavy pots and pans, but always available to pitch in and help.

She was a woods nymph, hardly coming up to my belt. Her long blonde hair bounced as she bounded about, her blue eyes reflected the innocence of her being, and her tinkling laughter added brilliant joy to the wilderness setting. The guests adored her and even the tame camp deer seemed to delight in trotting along behind her.

Her humor became an enlightening trap. One by one she cornered guests and played on their grownup personalities. With deliberate measured speech and careful pronunciation of each word she approached them.

"Have you heard the latest knock-knock joke?" she'd ask. "Here is how it goes – you start it."

The guest would grin, sit down, fold their hands, and give her their full attention.

"Okay honey," they'd say. "Knock, knock."

Then she would stand peering straight into them.

"Who's there?" she'd reply.

The guest would stutter – confounded. Then realize they'd been had by the youngest of sly comic geniuses and roar at their predicament.

At night she curled up in her sleeping bag beside me, unconcerned about the grizzly bears and cougars that hunted in the darkness.

During the day we rode along the streams and mountain trails. We hiked to the glacial Sock Lake atop the Chinese Wall, and lunched in a meadow at the confluence of Rock Creek and the Sun River.

Throughout the trip, her bursts of happiness and bubbling dialogue healed a spot in me that hurt too long. The sun shined brighter and the sky was deeper and bluer.

Years have passed. The daily grind wears at a person's soul. But a cowboy's soul is hard to hog-tie, and I'm especially lucky. On a drizzly mountain morning, looking into my daughter's teary eyes, the love of my life came home. I don't ride through life lost or alone anymore.

So, whether it's Valentines, Christmas, a birthday, or any other day of the year – every daddy should pay notice to the special person who follows his tracks up the trail.

Eight Days in Heaven

D ay 1: It's an easy ride into the mountains. The weather is pleasant, and my horse steps out like he's feeling good. My string of mules follow, keeping a crisp pace.

The six hunters are typical, anxious office dwellers anticipating the wilderness experience and fearing it at the same time. They jabber with a restricted, constrained pleasantness. They arrived in three groups of two and are strangers to each other.

The stiff white canvas wall tents are a soul-pleasing sight - like coming home. Then something else makes me smile. Buzz Johnson, our camp tender, is asleep on the woodpile.

The cook has coffee on and our friend, Russ Barber, is in camp.

Buzz wakes up bleary-eyed and his nose is swollen and red. He gives everyone a rubber-lipped welcome and resigns to his cot. He's been into the snakebite medicine and had an allergic reaction.

That night at the supper table a couple of the hunters mutter some disgruntled foolishness about having a lackey from the bars in Choteau doing our camp chores.

We ignore them.

Day 2: The hunters gobble breakfast and jerk together their essentials for the day. Not much conversation circulates and everyone bustles around in a business-like manner. The guides huddle and discuss their individual hunting plans. Buzz serves coffee, and Russ laughs and keeps the atmosphere happy around the breakfast table.

By dark that evening the group is back in camp. The hunters are beginning to figure out the camp routines and they're turning their tents into comfortable nests. Buzz shows them how to care for their woodstoves and arrange their gear.

Nobody shot anything but everyone saw either deer or elk.

The supper table is a little friendlier, and Buzz even sneaks into a few of the conversations.

Day 3: The hunters eat breakfast and notice how good the food is. They fret over dry socks and the useless gear they could have left at home. The guides huddle and make their daily war plans.

That evening the hunters go home to their nests and then ease over to lounge at the cook tent.

The conversation is more relaxed and easy, and some of the hunters are curious about Russ and Buzz. Everyone compliments the cook after supper.

Day 4: Breakfast goes well, but there is mumbling amongst the hunters about a general lack of game in the area. Russ and Buzz appease the clients while the guides make new war plans. Everyone thanks the cook for a great breakfast.

At supper there is a discussion about game populations in wilderness areas. The outfitter and Buzz do most of the talking.

The hunters are confused about Buzz. They can't quite figure him out.

Day 5: An empty meat pole doesn't make for a happy camp. Breakfast has a tight-lipped feeling about it. Everyone is civil and the guys are becoming a unified group, but something good needs to happen.

Today the outfitter and his hunter bag an elk, and one of my hunters gets a mule deer. The guides take care of getting the meat to camp, and a celebration is in progress by the time we finish our work.

But, the hunters are embarrassed – somebody finally found out – Russ is the local Methodist preacher... the party continues.

Day 6: Hunting camp works its magic and makes the full transformation. More meat goes on the pole and everyone is in tune.

Three hunters crowd around Buzz mesmerized by his discussion of mutual funds, municipal bonds and T-bills. He expounds on the history of Montana Power and the electric power industry, and then continues with a lecture of his political views.

The hunters are relaxed. There is no contact with the outside world and the problems of the office are secondary.

Today there is more talk about home and family.

Day 7: The last day of the hunt is also successful if for no other reason than because everyone has become friends. Business cards are traded and the strangled constipated-looking faces that came to camp a week ago are once again human looking.

Everyone figured out Buzz. He is wonderful amalgam of contradictions who can fit equally at a Seattle opera black-tie premiere or split wood for the cook. He once owned and operated Montana Plumbing Supply. During WWII he walked across France and was with the first GIs to liberate the concentration camps. His wife is a professor at the university in Missoula, and they enjoy an annual train trip across Russia.

Day 8: There is some sadness when the hunters take their last look at camp. It's been a cleansing experience. Nevertheless, the guys are ready to go home. They look forward to seeing their wives. The problems that plagued them a week ago are simplified, or eliminated.

Some of them are going home with trophies. All of them are remembering the people and good things that make life worthwhile.

No Sweat

A hunting party of Blackfeet Indians rode out of the timber and onto the rim where I was standing. Time took a sudden leap backwards as seven Indian men rode up to me. We faced each other on an alpine ridge in the Bob Marshall Wilderness in northwestern Montana. We faced each other in the bigoted confines of our minds.

Each region of the U.S. historically has its own ethnic problems. With each generation racial prejudice, and the imagined reasons for it, slip further into the past. However, in the American West the wheels of progress need greasing. It is common knowledge American Indians haven't been welcomed in a lot of public establishments; and likewise whites are discouraged from entering clubs where redmen enjoy exclusivity. It hasn't been many years since a group of supposedly intoxicated Blackfeet men cornered a federal forest service ranger in Badger Cabin, on the Two Medicine River. Firing their rifles in the air, they demanded to be arrested for hunting without a license. Their sole purpose was to make a federal case about American Indians needing licenses to hunt federal land. However, wisely, the ranger locked himself in the cabin and did nothing. From his point of view, the red brothers weren't hunting – they were just bothering him.

Meanwhile, the hunting party I faced consisted of six younger guys and one old man. Nobody smiled. They just sat on their horses not talking, surveying the basin below – and me. My greeting was sincere and honest.

"Howdy, how y'all boys doing? Y'all had any luck seeing anything?"

They all looked at me surprised by my Texas accent. A long silent moment held us. Then the old man walked his horse towards me and began jabbering like an old farm woman lecturing her chickens.

The tension passed. A couple of the boys dug their lunches out of their saddlebags, and sat on the ledge enjoying the sunshine.

The day was warming up and I had too many clothes on. The hunt started in the freezing darkness before sunrise, but now it was nearing noon. My thermal underwear needed to come off. The old man continued yabbering as his protégés studied the mountain valley.

I hooked a toe behind my heel and slipped off a hunting shoe and stood on it. Then I did the same with the other foot and stood on top of my shoes not letting my socked feet get in the dirt. The old bird seemed not to notice. I hung my coats on a tree and reached for my gunbelt. Seven pairs of eyes slanted to watch me. I took off the pistol and hung it beside my coats. Then I systematically undressed. First I took off my heavy flannel shirt and then my jeans. Then I peeled off my longjohns. The process was a balancing act, never stepping off the tops of my hunting shoes.

Some of the boys watched until they realized the final result. The others smirked and tried to concentrate on something in the distance. The poor old man was stuck talking to me, and had a sick frustrated look on his face.

In the crystal air of a wilderness afternoon I traumatized that hunting party from the reservation.

I stripped down naked, except for the BVDs I'd been wearing for six days, and never missed a word of the conversation.

That night, in the cook tent, I mentioned my run-in with a Blackfeet hunting party. The hunters sat quiet as implications of what I said sank in. The outfitter gave me a concerned look and asked what I'd done.

"Aw hell, I just took off all my clothes and let 'em know I wasn't a-scared."

There are two morals to this wonderful little story.

One is that prejudice is a fabrication of the mind; skin us down and we're all pretty much the same.

The other is that even if you're one lonely cowboy surrounded by a bunch of frowning Indians, never let 'em see you sweat.

Slow on the Draw – But Always Ready

The young lady had a contemptuous glare in her eye. She was a sporty little dishwater blonde with a white smile and a fast figure. At the moment, she was acting female. She was being snide and challenging as she gasped with mock horror.

"You have a gun on," she said. "Why are you wearing a gun, do you plan to kill something?"

Eight of her peers stood behind her. Their concern seemed to be more genuine.

"No ma'am, I don't plan on killing anything."

She cut me off short. She was snapping her words in a nasal tone and wanted to win her point.

"Then why are you carrying it? Do you need it, or do you wear it just for show?"

I smiled at her. I wasn't going to let this child get my goat.

"One reason I keep it handy is because sometimes bear come into camp."

"Oh, so if a bear comes into camp you're going to kill it?"

"No ma'am, I'll try to run him off cussing at him but if that doesn't work I'll shoot over his head. So far, that's always worked in the past. I've never killed anything in the mountains with my pistol. I carry it to keep critters out of camp, or to signal lost hunters. I've been lucky I've never needed it for an up-close personal visit with a grizz, but I guess that's always a possibility," I said. Then I cut myself short to prevent a soapbox speech.

The young lady stood silent as she processed my words into her cute cluttered think-box. Then she seemed to relax and I could see that she'd decided it was all right for me to wear my gun. Maybe she was even a little relieved. The rest of the group also seemed to accept the idea that my job was to protect and guide them.

We were headed into the Bob Marshall Wilderness for a summer pack trip along the Sun River. The first leg of the trip had us riding over one of the highest passes in the backcountry, Headquarters Pass. Our guests were nine girls from a girl's school in Massachusetts. They all seemed to be city-raised kids ranging in age from 14 to 22; and coming from a democrat state, I didn't blame them for having misconceptions about real life.

I never mentioned to the girls that my pistol was worn up-front, while the other mule packer, Tom, kept a sawed off shotgun concealed in his bedroll.

The trail ascending Headquarters Pass is a steep wind-blown path to God. A rider leaves the treeline and continues up through the barren rocky escarpments. There are places where a step off the trail would mean a thousand-foot drop.

The headwaters of the Teton River spring from solid rock at the summit and spiderweb down across smooth granite until it becomes a stream. Looking up at the crisscrossing lines of water on the rock face slanted against the high outline of the peaks and the eternity of deep blue sky beyond, can cause a rider to cling to the saddlehorn to fight vertigo.

Camp was hidden in a beautiful narrow valley on Gates Creek. The mountainsides were greenhouses of timber and grass. The livestock didn't need to go far to stand and graze in belly-deep forage. But the rascals liked to travel the mile to the Gates Park Ranger Station and graze along the airstrip. The grass on the edges was short, tender, and sweet. Having this knowledge made it easy to keep track of the remuda.

The airstrip was used only for extreme emergencies and to fight fires.

The Gates Park Ranger Station is also within the Sun River Game Preserve. There is no hunting allowed from the Sun River to the continental divide.

The gaggle of young ladies turned camp into home and living in the rugged conditions became second nature.

A summer thunderstorm rolled in one evening while Tom and I were rounding up the livestock. We rode towards the airstrip and watched the foggy wet clouds move down the hillsides towards us. Tom's blue-heeler cow dog came along for company and trotted between the horses. Thunder rumbled and boomed about the mountaintops with such severity that it interrupted our conversations.

Suddenly my horse leaped sideways and I heard Tom's dog yipe. I looked down in disbelief. A coyote had come between the horses and attacked the blue-heeler, and the attack was still on.

I jerked down my rope and went after him. The coyote circled and went back after the dog. The chase took us through a stand of quakie trees and into a swampy wash. My horse started lunging and nearly bogged down. The dog kept trying to get to the safety of the horses and the coyote kept trying to get between the horses and the dog. The second time I was almost unseated I'd had enough.

I stepped off my horse and pulled my pistol.

The dog ducked behind us and the coyote stopped and stared.

Rain began to pelt us harder and thunder blasted and reverberated against the mountains. Then the bottom dropped out and it poured.

I remounted and we rode to the ranger's station.

The forest service ranger came out to meet us, and he gave me a questioning gaze.

"This is a heck of a thunder-boomer ain't it? Say, you didn't have problems with a coyote did you? I had one get after my dog the other day. That's what happens when these critters don't get hunted and lose respect for people," he said.

"Yeah, we saw him," I said. "If you see him again, he probably won't be so sassy."

"Good," the ranger said.

Tom and I rode back and gathered the herd.

We took the group of girls back to the trailhead to conclude their trip, and headed to town for some rest and relaxation.

Our first stop was at the grocery store in Dupuyer for beer and barbecue chips. Then when we got to Choteau we stopped at the taxidermy shop and the feed store.

We were doing chores at the house when Tom stopped and looked at me.

"Are you going to sleep with that thing on?" he asked.

"What thing?" I asked.

"Your gun."

I felt by my side. The pistol was still there. I'd been all over town and nobody had ever noticed or said a word. I took it off and threw it on the truck seat.

Smiles Only Allowed in the Cook Tent

I felt content. The hunters were finishing their first supper in camp. The group had rode in during the afternoon, and one of the clients shot a mule deer buck the first evening. Everyone seemed happy, but saddle sore.

The hunter I would be guiding was an older gentleman. He had an easy smile, and his manner indicated character and class. He had hunted backcountry before and said he'd never hunt a private ranch as long as there was wilderness. I was looking forward to a week in the mountains with him.

Then someone spoke behind me.

"Herman, can I talk to you a minute?" asked another hunter.

I got up from the table to face the man.

"I didn't buy a wilderness hunt and come all the way to Montana to be guided by a lawyer from Ohio," the man said. He was sweating and looked perturbed.

The remark stabbed me. I was shocked. My first reaction was stuttering, but then the heat under my collar began to rise. He was referring to my good friend, Bill Taylor.

Bill knew the country as well as I did. He'd come to these mountains years ago. He began his association with us as a guest and graduated to being a guide. He is soft-spoken and even-tempered. His horsemanship, hunting, and guiding skills are beyond question. Such a callous slur could cut him to the quick.

I studied the client. It was my job to satisfy all the guests. He was the same five-feet-ten-inches as me, but outweighed me by 80 pounds. His meaty face was flushed crimson, and a marbled roll of fat protruded beneath his jowls. The cigarettes in his shirt pocket explained his body odor and wheezing breath. His clothes were expensive, however, his statement showed poor taste and a lack of judgment. I decided Mother Nature and the natural selection process had missed eliminating this specimen.

But I answered in a subdued voice.

"Well sir, you'd have a good hunt with Bill. He's a smart hunter and knows the country. He'll be horseback more than I will. If you hunt with me, you'll be doing a lot of walking. We all know where the critters are supposed to be, but we each have different styles of hunting. I like to get up high where I can look around. Horses can't climb where I go."

The malcontent puffed out his cheeks and whined.

"The outfitter told me – you do most of your hunting from horses."

"Yeah well – sort of. I may ride a couple of miles from camp and tie up. Then I'll walk a five or six mile circle, stopping in my favorite spots to glass."

Then a mean thought struck me.

"I bet the outfitter told you we all know CPR too. But the truth is, it wouldn't do you any good this far back in the hills. The best we could do is try to keep one of our endangered species from eating you before fetching the body with a mule. We can cover a corpse with branches to stop eagles from eating you, but that wouldn't stop a grizzly. Nope, we'd be sending home pieces."

I wondered if any self-respecting grizz would eat this bloated rascal.

"The biggest reason you need to hunt with Bill is because he's got luck. I've got to work for what I get – Bill stumbles over more game by accident than I do on purpose. You've heard of lucky fishermen – Bill has that kind of luck hunting. Elk walk up to him while he's eating lunch."

The hunter shuffled his feet and peered at the ground while this information tried to soak into the gray matter of his asphalt and yellow-lined brain. Then he nodded, muttered something about giving Bill a chance, and waddled out of the tent.

I watched the over-pampered crybaby leave.

Bill's work was cut out for him. I pitied him.

I looked back to the older gentleman. He was seated, looking down at the table, chuckling to himself.

Good Things Come to Good People

J ohnny got off the plane and walked into the Great Falls airport. He looked excited, but bothered. We met and shook hands.

"Willie, I don't know about this," Johnny said.

"Don't worry, John, I'll help you. This is going to be an easy deal," I said. We gathered his luggage and I explained the situation.

The outfitter was shorthanded. He needed another guide, and at this late date, any warm body would do. I knew Johnny could help with livestock, camp chores, and do some guiding. The outfitter had confidence in my judgment. So, he hired Johnny via telephone and sent him a one-way plane ticket from Houston to Great Falls.

Some of the local Montana boys were skeptical. One of my mule packing buddies started the sarcasm.

"So, you want to be a great Rocky Mountain hunting guide, eh?" he asked.

Johnny and I ignored such remarks. But I was a little concerned about Johnny's physical condition. Living on the Texas Gulf Coast and having a job that involves pointing and telling others what to do, isn't in line with living in the Montana wilderness.

Two days later, we were in the hills putting up camp. Johnny caught on quick to the woodsman's camp duties, and while he was enjoying mountain life, I spent seven days packing in hay.

Then, Howard Henson, and Keith Schobel, from Columbus, Texas, flew up and rode into the mountains. The next five days we skidded logs to camp, crosscutting, and splitting them for firewood.

Finally, we had a day to take a tour and look over the hunting country. We rode up onto Crystal Ridge. From the north end, I could show Johnny our entire hunting area. We would hunt out of each other's way, but never far apart.

Then we rode towards the next point. It was a tough pull for the horses, so I tied up half-way and took off on foot. Keith and Howard fell in behind with Johnny bringing up the rear. We joked and I told stories as we climbed.

Then I heard a thud. Johnny was lying on the ground. He was huffing and puffing and couldn't suck enough air.

"Johnny, you okay?" I asked.

"Yeah, Willie y'all go on... I can't make it," he said.

We were near the top.

"No John, this is where I want you to hunt. You're going to make this climb first thing in the morning - in the dark - and you need to get to the top," I said.

He looked at me like I'd been eating off the ground in the horse pen. Then he realized I was serious.

"This is a hell of a spot, John. You get to the top, then go down this other ridge. There's no telling what you'll see," I said.

He gathered himself and struggled to the top. Then we all took a break. The rest of the afternoon was spent lazying around near the sky, feeling like four Huckleberry Finns of the wilderness. When the first day of the hunting season came, Johnny and I were ready.

Johnny had the most essential ingredients for guiding. He was excited about his work. He's got the universal gift of gab, and he knew his first duty was to make sure his hunter was happy.

Despite our positive outlook, I knew the local boys were still snickering and passing around smart aleck comments.

The first day of the hunt, Johnny took his hunter to the north end of Crystal Ridge. They came back that evening babbling with stories. I watched them jabber and knew they were getting along.

The rest of the week went without a hitch. Everyone was seeing elk, but couldn't connect. The weather was mild and camping was easy. Johnny and his hunter finally stumbled onto a nice mule deer buck. Then one of my guys got lucky, and the first thing you know, the meat pole was practically full.

On the last evening Johnny's hunter called him to his tent. I already knew what was going to happen and hid where I could watch. The man talked to my friend, shook his hand, then reached inside and pulled out his Weatherby rifle. He tried to hand it to Johnny, but the guide didn't understand. The hunter said something else and Johnny hesitantly reached for the gun. The hunter clapped him on the shoulder and shook his hand again. Then Johnny turned and walked to the crew tent.

"I just got a Weatherby rifle for a tip," he said.

I smiled. I knew this would shut-up the local boys.

Size Doesn't Always Matter

The two men were a study in human nature. One of them was a slight, semi-bald old man. He had a quick smile, but his hearing was bad and his vision was questionable. He puttered around the mountain camp trying to listen to everyone's conversations and gain clues about the hunting. He handled himself like a man who had worked with his hands all his life. When you talked to him, his eyes looked straight into your face and you knew that he was an honest man. I guessed his age at about 75.

My first impression was that his partner was his grandson. The younger man was a typical 20-something-year-old with the exuberance and health associated with that age group. He wasn't a big guy and seemed to be made from the same mold as the older man. His short light-colored hair made him appear even younger. He settled into the subtle habits of camp life and it was plain to see that his main concern was the welfare of his older companion. It was reasonable he moved with the same mannerisms as the old man; he was his son.

Guiding a pair of hunters like this is a trick. Wilderness hunts can be the experience of a lifetime, and I knew that was what these two guys wanted.

On the other hand, backcountry hunts can be torturous and disappointing. There was no way that the older hunter was going to get an elk unless one stumbled over him. So, for the first few days I tried to make that happen.

There were a few spots that a blessed hunter may catch an elk doodling along a hillside, it's rare but it is possible. However, to get to these spots we had to climb into stiff frozen saddles and ride for an hour-and-a-half before daylight.

We'd leave ol' Dad under a tree where he could watch a good chunk of country while junior and I walked the ridges and glassed from the high spots. We'd get back to our starting point around lunchtime and move Dad to another spot and then take off on a different loop to check out some more country.

My plan wasn't working. After a couple of days without seeing game I had to come up with a new idea. Besides, they weren't enjoying all that saddleback time in the dark.

"Boys, we're going to have to hunt a little closer to camp," I said. "There are a lot of mule deer above camp, up towards the continental divide. I can put Pops in a spot where he's sure to at least see deer while we get on top and look for elk."

The idea suited everybody fine.

The next morning my hunters enjoyed their flapjacks and biscuits a little longer and I had an extra couple of cups of coffee. A few minutes before dawn we mounted up and rode the short mile to the horse pasture.

Again I put the older fellow in a likely spot while junior and I took a little hike.

"The hardest thing about hunting these deer is waiting on a good one," I said.

Junior gave me a puzzled look.

"Well, there are a lot of little guys and not many mature bucks. We'd like to see the young bucks walk and have our hunters go home with a good trophy." I said. "It's better for the deer herd, and I'd rather spend my time packing trophies out of the mountains than the little dinks."

The boy looked at the ground and dug a toe in the dirt before replying.

"Dad can't see that good. If he thinks it's got horns he's going to shoot," he said.

As if on cue, we heard ol' Pops cut loose with his rifle. We listened to the shot echo through the mountains. Then we started back. I had a bad feeling.

The old man was in the spot where we'd left him, and he was still watching deer. His shot had been a miss but the deer hadn't spooked. Four young bucks and a handful of does and fawns were on the adjacent hillside.

The old man was breathing hard.

"Get over here. I think I got one. They haven't left, maybe you can get a shot at one," the old man said to the boy.

"Hold up, that's a long shot. Let's see what we've got before we do anymore shooting," I said.

The deer had gotten leery and they did the typical exiting mule deer stiff-legged bounce up the hill. Junior and I left Pops in his spot and went to look for blood.

While we were looking for sign the boy explained the situation to me.

"Dad just wants to have a good hunt. He doesn't care so much about trophies. He hasn't killed a deer in several years and we'll probably never make a hunt like this again," he said.

I looked at the young man and had mixed emotions about what he was telling me. We sat under a tree and had a good heart-to-heart visit.

The next morning I took the two to the same place and left them. They sat close together under a small lone pine and behind some low buck brush. They huddled near each other whispering and watching. From a distance, I looked at the two hunters and the scene looked right.

I returned to camp to cut wood, feed horses and do whatever chores the cook hadn't done. But before I could get started, a shot sounded from the horse pasture.

I caught a mule and headed back to the place where I'd left the hunters. I knew what I was going to see when I got there – and I was right.

That afternoon the same thing happened again. I smiled and congratulated my hunters and never mentioned again that we were trying to save the young deer.

That night we had a happy camp. A father and son were successful hunters and their mountain pack trip was the experience they desired.

It was my job to see that the hunters were happy, not to curtail their pleasure with my standards of trophy hunting and herd management.

I felt sorry about the young deer.

But seeing the closeness of the father and son that were separated by 50-some-odd years was enough to humble me. I didn't have the right to throw a ripple in their happiness, and I didn't.

Loving Something You Can't Have

The day started before the sun came up. The canvas wall tents were illuminated by gas lanterns but ten steps away the blackness swallowed a person. Tired hunters shuffled to breakfast dodging piles of firewood, axes, and saws stacked beside the cook tent. I stood under a tree, in the dark watching the scene, trying to guess where the elk were. I faced the westerly breeze, and a cold mist chilled my skin. Then I turned and went into the tent where everyone was gathering.

"No horses today, we're walking," I said to my hunter.

Val Johnson sat at the long table cleaning up a plateful of fried eggs. He hunkered over his tin plate like a small bear and nodded his head in agreement. Val is a good man, a Vietnam veteran, and a good hunter.

It was the last day of the early elk season and I needed to find him a bull. It was the second year Val was hunting with us. He shot a fine mule deer buck the year before but had gotten no elk. Earlier this week I'd found him another good mule deer buck. But now, I was running out of time for an elk.

We left camp walking like ducks-on-ice down the creek bank and across the log footbridge. Then we hiked to the valley called the "Lunchbox." The sky threatened us, but we never saw it as we entered the cavernous timber.

The trail became steep and muddy and our walk turned into a slippery trudge. We approached the first meadow and waited for daylight – nothing happening. We marched farther up the trail, and then the sky dumped its load. Big sploshy snowflakes soaked us as the temperature dropped. In moments visibility was only a few yards, and our clothes began to freeze.

We were on the eastern rim of the valley, and hunting was impossible in the storm - just as I'd planned.

I followed a shallow depression that led into a stand of spruce. Beneath a giant spruce was my old campfire spot. A cache of wood was piled against the tree. Val wiped and shook the snow from his clothes, and I began to build a fire. The surrounding trees protected us from the weather as if we were in a house.

The next few hours we luxuriated by the fire. If you can't see you can't hunt, so we sat in our green alcove, enjoying the warm flames, nibbling on our lunches, and sharing our innermost thoughts. Val sat on a log and periodically got up to check the weather. I sat on the ground with my legs stretched out and my back against the spruce tree.

At 1:00 p.m. the storm broke. Once again we could look down into the "Lunchbox" – nothing happening.

We followed the main trail up a short steep climb, and looked east towards Big Horn Mountain.

Big Horn Mountain is in the Rand McNally Atlas, 30 miles west of Bynum, Montana.

We surveyed the scattered timber on the broad mountainside. Then something moved. We stepped behind cover and raised our binoculars. Then, whispering, we counted.

Ten cow elk grazed on the hillside three-quarters of a mile away, and as we watched the wheels were spinning in my head.

"The bull is down below, in the timber," I said. "But the cows are drifting towards the south. They're headed to a little pass. We can skirt around to the top, then turn east and drop down to where they're going. If we hurry we can catch the bull when he comes through the pass."

Val agreed.

Forty-five minutes later we were there. We couldn't see the elk, but we could cover the pass where they were supposed to show up. So, we waited.

The clouds dissipated, and the sun worked on the fresh snow. We waited.

Small birds began working through the stunted trees and the afternoon shadows grew. We waited.

Snow dripped from the trees and patches of green showed where minutes before there had been a complete blanket of snow. I couldn't stand it anymore.

"Let's go find them damn elk!"

We took off at a trot - back to where we had started.

There they were. The first one I saw was a big fat cow with horns. I did a double-take. The cows were farther up the mountain. The bull had finally come out of the bottom.

Val asked the obvious.

"How do we get to him?"

I stood there shaking my head.

"Ain't no way... There's too much brush to go straight at him. The cows have us cut off from making a sneak from the top. I don't know what the wind is doing over there, and none of it matters because it's going to be dark before we get to him anyway."

Val mulled this over for quite awhile. His expression didn't change. He looked at the scene. Then he relaxed and sat on the ground.

The season ended for us that afternoon. We sat watching the bull with his herd of ten cows. The animals were in good shape and their buckskin hides shined blue in the late autumn afternoon. The bull's antlers glinted in the sunlight and he was king of the mountains. Val smiled.

"I don't know anyplace I'd rather be. The sight of that bull with his cows will be something I'll be able to remember anytime... anywhere..." Val said.

I looked at my hunter and nodded. Here was a man that loved to put meat in the freezer and horns on the wall. But this trophy wasn't going on the wall. This was a defining moment we would both carry in our hearts – a time and place to relive whenever life gets too hard.

The Everlasting Elk Hunter

The gas lanterns lit the inside of the canvas tents and camp was a happy place. The cook handed out plates of flapjacks and bacon with fried eggs. Everything was fried in bacon grease and tasted great.

The hunters were a group of older gentleman, and they were anxious. It was going to be hard to follow my plan. We sat facing each other across the long breakfast table. The horses had been caught, fed, and saddled.

"Now look guys," I said. "We've got good hunting right out of camp. There's no point in riding out of here in the pitch dark. I'd like to be able to see a little when we get to the horse pasture and that's only fifteen minutes up the trail."

The horse pasture is an open side of a mountain that runs up to the continental divide. The outfitter gave me a dubious look.

"You actually expect to see elk in the horse pasture? What are the chances of that?" he asked.

"Well, there were elk on the backside of that mountain a week ago and we haven't bothered them. They may not be standing in the middle of the horse pasture, but I'm hoping they're still around," I said.

My argument appeased them for only a few minutes. Then the general conversation drifted back towards the need of getting into the woods. I walked in circles as if I was gathering my gear, and delayed leaving as long as I could. I looked at my watch and hid in the crew tent, but they rousted me out. Finally, I couldn't put them off any longer.

I doodled around getting them mounted, and still – we got on the trail more than an hour before sunrise.

The three men that followed me were well educated, well groomed, professional businessmen. They loved the wilderness camps and living the old way – fetching water from the creek, cutting firewood with a crosscut saw, and eating good cholesterol-soaked food.

We rode through the woods without speaking. When we reached the horse pasture I stopped and tried to see through the darkness. I strained my ears listening, and rode ahead one slow step at a time.

Then suddenly something stampeded in front of me. I stared hard. I could barely discern the large buckskin rumps racing away in front of me – elk. I cussed!

The only thing to do was continue. I decided to go a little farther. I'd go to the top of Crystal Ridge. Hopefully, we hadn't spooked the elk out of the country.

I put the first old gentleman, Walt, at the north end of the ridge. He could look down into the timber where the elk had avoided us. Then I took the second hunter midway down the ridge where he could watch the pass between Gateway Creek and the East Fork of Strawberry Creek. I took my third guest to the south end where he could watch the grass-covered slope and the valley on the backside of the ridge. The horses had been tied at daylight, and by the time I walked back to my first hunter it was midmorning.

"Well, have you seen anything?" I asked.

"Yeah, a whole bunch of elk walked through the opening right below me," he said. He pointed to a wide opening 150 yards beneath the spot where he was seated.

I thought this was reasonable, but there had to be more to the story.

"No bulls?" I asked.

He gave me a sheepish look.

"Yeah, I saw a bull but I didn't get a shot," he said.

I looked down at the meadow and wondered how a bull could cross that expanse of open grass without offering a shot.

Walt explained.

"Well, a cow came out and walked all the way across. Then another cow came out. I watched her and followed her in my riflescope. She went into the timber and I was still trying to see her when a bull walked through my scope while I was looking to see where the cow went," he said. "It surprised me, and he was walking pretty fast so I never got a shot."

I was dumfounded. Here seemed to be a real city dude who durn sure needed a guide to hold his hand and tell him when to shoot.

The day didn't get any better. One of my other hunters missed a bull, and the other one didn't see anything at all.

I spent the entire eight-day hunt working tenaciously to find a good trophy and put my hunters in chip shot range. It was exasperating to me, but my guests stayed in good spirits. They didn't demand too much of me and knew that I was doing my best. They were fun camp companions, helped wash dishes, and enjoyed cocktails and stimulating conversations at night.

On the last day Walt approached me.

"Now Herman, if I had shot that bull the first morning – what would I tell my wife when I want to come back next year?" he asked.

We looked at each other eye-to-eye and he smiled at me. I've never known if he let that bull walk on purpose or if he botched the shot. But Walt has been hunting elk for 17 years and he hasn't killed one yet.

~ CHRISTMAS ~

A Cowboy Christmas Story

It's cold this morning. In fact it's bitter cold, and saddling my wrangle pony at 3:30 a. m. is no pleasant chore. I've got to go up on the mountain, and bring in the riding stock for the day's hunt. The stock must be fed and saddled for our guests by daylight. It's a daily activity of hunting camp which normally takes two to three hours, but can take longer. My disposition can be pretty sour this time of the day, until I get into the saddle, and then everything seems to improve.

It's a little better than a mile to the mountainside that serves as our horse pasture. I truly enjoy this job, even though I grumble about it. I especially enjoy this duty on early mornings like today. It's clear weather, though during the night we had four inches of fresh snow. The stars are shining magnificently and I can ride out of camp without using a flashlight. The evergreen trees are a beautiful crystalline white, practically magical world, and me and my ol' pony are making the first tracks in this postcard scene. By the time I'm half way up the trail, I've forgotten the cold, and I'm completely entranced by my surroundings. The ride is invigorating, and at the base of the mountain, another amazing sight awaits me. The Northern Lights shoot and dance over the top of the mountain, and for many long moments I sit on my ol' pony with my mouth hanging open.

Well, it's time to go to work, and bring in the horses. To find them, we put bells on about a half-dozen of them. So, normally you'll hear 'em long before you see 'em, and quite often you'd never find 'em if not for the bells. This particular day I ride half way up the open mountain side straining my ears trying to pick up the clang of a bell, and par for the course, I hear the rascals plumb at the top. This requires me to ride as far as I can, but then because of the steep slope, I'm forced to dismount and climb on foot leading my mount. It's a particular pain in the butt to bring 'em down off the top; and the remuda seems to enjoy making a feller have to do it. Naturally, I do my standard cussing procedure, and begin my climb.

Now, something is definitely wrong. I've gotten high enough that I can hear a long way, and I'm hearing more bells from the west of me. This creates a new problem, and I have to sit down a minute, catch my breath, and cipher this out.

Due west of me is Crystal Ridge. It's a high rock ridge about two miles long. It's flat and smooth on top and I have found our livestock grazing there. However, normally they don't split up this bad. It's at least a mile between where I hear the two groups of bells, something must have spooked the herd causing it to scatter. This fact works on my curiosity and I head for Crystal Ridge, watching for some type of predator tracks on the way. It takes the best part of 45 minutes to pick my way down one high spot and up another.

Now, I've noticed something peculiar about this second set of bells. They seem to chime for awhile, and then drift off. Then, there are moments I can't hear 'em at all, and then all of a sudden, I can hear 'em just louder than hell, only to have them drift off again. It's a confusing but curious situation.

Finally, I ride up over the ridge. There in the starlight, I survey the high open expanse – and there's nothing there. At least, first observation is producing nothing. No bells, no horses, not a single sound or living creature – just total stillness. Now, I'm really fouled up. Then I spot an oddity in the snow, riding forward along the escarpment .

Holy Jehosaphat! My ol' bronc swallows his head, and blows sideways like his life depends on it. I manage to weather that move but something whooshes over our heads. And the elusive bells are back. I feel like I'm riding broncs in a church steeple. I'm strung out too far. I was caught unexpecting, and that gentle pony's next couple of moves pile drives me – deep through the snow and head first into the ground. The back of my head and my toes hit terra firma at the same time with my backside pointed straight to the heavens. Boy, my bell is rung.

Eventually, I get myself untwisted, untangled, and lift my head out of the dirt. I get up brushing off caked snow. Mad, bewildered, and a little spooked I try to find the source of my problems.

Farther down the ridge I spot an object but can't discern its identity. Then I hear something that stops me dead in my tracks. Somebody is sitting down there chuckling. Then, in a loud voice that I haven't heard in thirty-some-odd years, I'm questioned.

"Herman Brune, you rascal, is that you?"

With a great frog in my throat I respond, "Yes Sir!"

"What in tarnation you doing up on this ridge, this time of the morning?"

"Well," I started to answer, but then got indignant remembering this ol' bird just got me bucked off my horse. So I questioned him a while.

"What in hell are you doing, playing around up here, causing me trouble?"

Seeing my ire, the ol' boy smiled and explained.

"This time of year I've got to oil my harnesses and knock some of the dust off the sleigh. I got to get these reindeer limbered up, too. They've been standing around getting fat all summer. You know, you can't expect 'em to cover the ground they cover in one night without some exercise, and warming up. I've been practicing take-offs and landings up on this ridge for years."

By this time I'd walked up to him and was leaning against his rig. Dasher and Dancer, and the rest of the team eyed me suspiciously, not accustomed to having a civilian so near. With a smile and a wink he reached under his seat and pulled out a bottle of Canadian whiskey.

"Here you go son, looks like after that pile-up I caused you could use a drink. Sorry about that little wreck, but temptation got the best of me. By the way, speaking of temptation, how many times you been married now? You sure ain't the sweet little Sunday school piano player you used to be. Fact is, I heard your last address was in a jail up around Dallas somewhere. You know, I don't deliver presents to no jail houses."

At this remark he caught a laughing fit and about rolled out of his sleigh.

Well, what could I say? He had me flat-footed but once more I came back at him.

"Listen here you ol' blustering coot, I've done a lot of mean things, and I enjoyed every damn one of 'em but you better not hold my sins against none of my little buddies. I've got a daughter that's sweeter than I ever could have been, and I've got a nephew that figures Uncle Herman is pretty neat. Most of my buddies got kids these days, and I've got a whole big pile of little pardners scattered between Mexico and Canada. For getting my head plowed into the ground you better be extra special nice to them children this year, or I'll come back on this ridge next year and make taxidermy out of them reindeer."

The ol' boy sat there and gave me sort of a wise look.

"Herman, you ain't near so tough as you'd like to sound. You might be a bad actor on occasion, but I believe I see why most kids like you. Don't worry about your little buddies, I'll take extra special good care of 'em this year. Now, quit leaning on my buggy, I got to get out of here. I've got to be getting home and give these ol' deer a good rub down".

I backed off, and he gave me another wink and a smile.

"Take care cowboy!"

In a rush his reindeer charged down the ridge. Then pulled off the ground and began making a wide loop. They circled back by me headed north and cupping my hands to my mouth I hollered, "Hey Santa, you gonna bring me anything for Christmas?"

With a robust true-hearted laugh that is common to cowboys and mountain men, he reached under his seat and tossed me a half-empty bottle of Canadian whiskey.

Then he disappeared into the stars.

I took another slug on the bottle, rubbed the knot on my head, and headed back to find my horse.

~ Resorts –
Destinations -
Outfitters ~

Mexico ~ to ~ Montana

Exotic Locales to Experience the Ultimate Fishing and Wing Shooting Adventures

- Mexico, Hacienda Don Quixote

The day blistered to life and the sun was a hazy yellow ball. We loaded our gear in the truck and motored south from McAllen, Texas. The air-conditioned cab provided cool respite, but the low flat buildings and the brown baked earth testified this is harsh country – hot red sifting sand and everything grows spines.

We crossed the international border at Reynosa and the landscape greened. Our route crossed the flourishing soils of the Rio Grande River Valley. Fresh crops reached into the Mexican spring air, while fat horses and cattle luxuriated in pastures of deep grass.

Our host, Don Turner, orated about his coming to Mexico but I only stared out the window. Recent structures, fallen stone fences, hand-painted plywood signs, and roadside fruitstands, bespoke a culture that screamed the more things change the more they stay the same.

The highway led us out of the valley and into the desert hills much akin to the Texas Hill Country. Yuccas, prickly pear, and wild persimmon camouflaged the barren rocks with tints of color and shaded the broken desert. Blue Mountains, the Sierra Madres, rose on the horizon fading and teasing like a mirage – but becoming ever nearer.

Then we turned from the pavement, and in a breath we left the desolate cactus covered hills and passed through the gates of a tiled plaza. We entered a tropical oasis paradise – a step away from reality – The Hacienda Don Quixote.

Smiling tuxedoed waiters stood poised with trays of margaritas and fanciful Mexican hors d'oeuvres. More staff hurried to carry our luggage to palapa-roofed cabanas hidden in a forest of giant ficus and palm trees.

A perpetual cool breeze and splashing cantera stone fountains sooth the courtyard. Banana, papaya, and mimosa trees seclude and subscribe privacy to the individual accommodations. Stone-paved paths wind through the leafy canopied tunnels of the garden connecting the living quarters and leading to an oversized bubbling hot tub.

The first morning we awoke in our new Shangri-la, we loaded into vans and headed to Lake Guerrero. I was told that even a poor fisherman like myself would be surprised at my success. But my initial shock came when I realized the lady I was fishing with had bragged about her abilities too soon. It seems her only practiced skill was untangling the bird nests out of her reel. However, at the end of the first morning she'd bested me by one fish. I assumed it was because I spent most of my time drinking beer and watching her cast in hopes the strained buttons on her shirt would pop open. Then, it was back to the hacienda, more margaritas, and into the hot tub.

The second day was a repeat of the first, and again at the end of the morning I'd been bested. The rest of the day went much the same, nothing but my fishing partner and I, and some lascivious play.

The third day we took a break and went shopping in Victoria, moving ever nearer the Sierra Madres. It was a good recess and an opportunity to see a city in the interior of Mexico. The market area is comparable to any mall if you're into watching people.

On the fourth day I was tired of being out-fished by a girl. I started trying. For a little while I was ahead by two and then in no time at all she caught three and I could see the evil gleam in her eye indicating she was about to make a complete ass out of me.

Then to my luck, she got tangled in some limbs beneath the surface. Like a gentleman, I offered to untangle her line and she demurely handed me her pole. I gave it a muscled jerk snapped the pole in half, and that was the end of the contest.

For everyone besides me, Lake Guerrero boasts having the best bass fishing in the world. Days of catching 50 or more fish are common, and the big fish range from eight to 14 pounds. The lake is a bass fisherman's dream. Set in the flooded foothills of the mountains, the depths of the lake have the natural structure to make bass prolific. The water level is the best it's been in years. It's a lake in which an inexperienced fishing novice or a weathered old pro can have a good time.

The largest white-wing dove colony in the world nests nearby. Biologists have estimated the population at two-and-one-half million birds and depending on the rain they may have two to three hatches a year. The government protects the nesting area, and conservation practices assure excellent dove hunting for years to come. The legal limit of 80 birds a day is reasonably possible.

The gentleman's sport of quail hunting covers an unlimited acreage and the hunting is unsurpassed. Busting 20 coveys of wild bobwhites a day is the norm. Guides handle the dogs and when dogs see that many quail everyday, they know what to do.

The duck and goose hunting is a surprise for first timers to Mexico. Guests can go to the blind in shorts and tennis shoes. The guides serve cappuccino and provide their clients with the most laid back waterfowl hunts they will ever be on.

The hacienda provides all the shotguns and shells needed to have an exceptional sportsman's day in the field.

The Hacienda Don Quixote renders the perfect romantic hideaway for couples, or wing shooting and fishing for couples who enjoy the outdoors together. It also caters to corporate groups and groups who appreciate quality outfitter service.

I looked around and realized I was in the "Garden of Eden" – then I started wondering about Adam's rib and glanced around for my fishing partner.

-Montana, The H Lazy 6 Ranch

An easy breeze rustles the tall grass. The foothills roll and hide the treasures of the ranch – in their folds are lakes brimming with monster trout.

Pronghorn antelope, mule deer, and elk wander and migrate across the buttes and ridges. Shaggy-shouldered buffalo plod along the grand open expanse grazing while the prairie grizzly lurks rooting and hunting through the brushy creek bottoms.

The Rocky Mountains rise up bordering the western side of the ranch, and Ear Mountain stands like a fortress overlooking the grasslands of the eastern front. Behind the first wall of peaks lies the Bob Marshall Wilderness, two million acres of backcountry that's as wild as the day God made it. To the north, lay Glacier National Park, the Blackfeet Reservation, and the Sweet Grass Hills of Canada.

A person can close his or her eyes and feel the history of the world evolving around them. Egg Mountain is nearby, home of the dinosaur eggs that ignited the Jurassic Park stories. From there, the sparsely populated plains stretch to the east, across the alkali badlands of the Missouri breaks, and on to the Dakotas.

This is the setting of the American frontier Charlie Russell and Frederick Remington depicted in their art. This is the country that inspired Will James to write *Smoky the Cowhorse*, and A.B. Guthrie Jr. to write his Pulitzer prize-winning, *The Way West*, along with *The Big Sky* and *The Covered Wagon*.

This is the land the rest of the world identifies as America. It's a wilderness edged by ranches and reservations, cowboys and Indians, buffalo and grizzly bear. It exemplifies a way of life, a western standard or code many dream of and few achieve – but you are here – and you know it's real.

The H Lazy 6 Ranch, owned and operated by Hank and Laura Bouma, is far from the centers of tourist activity. Great Falls, Montana is an hour and a half away on the plains to the east. Choteau, Montana, the nearest town, is 20 miles back down a gravel road to the juncture of U. S. Highways 287 and 89.

The amenities of the ranch mingle Old West taste with graces of modern convenience. The log lodge and cabins are spacious, solid, comfortable, and suitably arranged. Mounted heads of native big game are appropriate for the lodge as well as memorabilia from days gone by. There is also a pool table and fly shop. The ranch can provide all the needs for the novice fly caster. The dining room is situated so your view faces the mountains. It is a panoramic splendor equaled only by the Grand Tetons, Himalayas, or Alps.

Meals vary but some include ranch-raised beef and buffalo. Hank and Laura guarantee home-style cooking in elegant surroundings befitting the discerning trout angler.

The cabins are a short walk from the lodge, and the best fly-fishing imaginable is at your front door. When you wet your line, you will be joining the excitement shared by some of the best fly fisherman in the world.

Professional fly fisherman Michael Fong listed the H Lazy 6 Ranch as one of the top destinations in the U.S. for still water fishing in his <u>Inside Angler</u> magazine.

The ranch has been in <u>Fly Fishing Magazine</u> and films produced for Fox Northwest Sports and Columbia Country putting it on over 100 television stations throughout the Pacific Northwest. It has also been mentioned favorably in the consumer report card for the <u>Angling Report</u>.

Pro fly caster from New Zealand, Hugh McDowell, says this is one of the best fisheries in the world.

Orvis has also pledged to endorse the H Lazy 6 Ranch in this coming year.

There are five lakes to test your skills. Each lake is stocked to provide the optimum growth potential for individual trout species. There are rainbow, cutthroat, brown, and brook trout. The average catch is 16 to 18 inches, but there are good chances to tangle with the eight to 10 pound hogs that range up to 28 inches.

"It's much like bone fishing or sight casting," says Hank. "Fish cruise looking for food. In a lake, a fish that is sitting still isn't feeding. Ninety percent of the fish feed in water two to six feet deep. Big fish feed where the best food source is available."

From September 1, into November upland bird hunting can be added to the day's events. Sharp-tailed grouse and Hungarian partridge offer fast action wing shooting to compliment your Montana experiences.

"These are non-guided hunts, but we certainly take a hands-on approach to helping our guests," says Hank. "Bird hunters will realize the quality of hunting private land versus competing with the public."

Then, if a horseback excursion is required to fulfill your vacation – checkout Laura Bouma's dad, Chuck Blixrud, at the 7 Lazy P. He's been a backcountry outfitter for 40 years, and has catered to such notables as cosmetic mogul Liz Claiborne.

Six-time repeat customer, Jack Burke, from Billings, Montana sums it up.

"The eye of the camera cannot capture everything this ranch has to offer," says Burke. "A person has to be here to appreciate this country."

The Garden of Eden was created for all of man's comforts, and humans continuously strive to recreate it.

The Rocky Mountains are God's Cathedral.

Respect Breeds Respect

- Austria

The red stag made the stunned jump that comes after a lung shot. Then it wobbled downhill a few steps and collapsed, rolled over, kicked a few times and was done. The young guide, or revierjager, smiled and shook his hunter's hand. They both spoke at the same time without hearing each other, too excited about the collection of a fine trophy. The guide congratulated his client with the traditional Austrian "weidmanns heil." The hunter responded with the traditional "weidmanns dank," but his voice twanged with a Texas accent uncommon to the Austrian Alps.

The hunt was taking place in Radurschal Tal, an alpine valley in the three corners region of Austria. Italy was within walking distance, and Switzerland was only a short drive away. It was two weeks before the "brunft," (rut).

The guide and hunter left their concealed position and picked their way across a stream and up the hill. They both walked around the stag, but the guide only stood to admire it for a second. He continued to a nearby pine tree and broke off three branches. One he placed in the stag's mouth and called it "letzer bissen" (last bite). Another branch he dipped in the blood on the side of the stag and then stuck it in the right side of the hunter's hat. This one he called "schutzen bruch." The last branch he left lying on the side of the stag covering the wound. This one he called "inbesitznahme bruch."

Later the stag was brought to camp on a "hornschlitter" or horn sled. It was delivered whole, and laid on its right side. A hunter, who was familiar with the tradition of "Tots" (totes), took his jagh horn and played the bugle call that honors the red hirsch (red stag). That was followed with a series of happy weidmanns heils and a round of schnapps for everyone.

That night supper was served at a restaurant owned by Seppl Haueis. On the walls of the dining room were rows of European mounts of roe deer and chamois. Before the meal Seppl introduced his father. The older gentleman greeted the party with a hearty weidmanns heil and handshakes around the table.

"My father is ninety years old. He took his last chamois from the high country when he was eighty-five. This year he got a roe deer," Seppl said.

The party laughed and smiled and another series of weidmanns heils and handshakes went around the table. The old man's face glowed and good-hearted feelings radiated from him like they do from a grandfather. Good-hearted feelings warmed the room - like they do in a good camp.

The people of Austria are genuine and honest. They take pride in their country and they have a deep respect for their natural resources and wildlife. They are heaped in history and traditions. They are much like the people of rural America two or three generations ago. They know that nothing comes without hard work and dedication.

Many of the industries have been in operation for hundreds of years and are still owned and operated by the originating families. This is true of the Gassmeyer Bell Co. Their first bell was produced in 1599.

The folks in Austria are gracious hosts. They greeted us with open, honest handshakes and hearts. They will sit down and systematically explain their traditions and ways of life. They will explain their hunting methods and the wildlife management practices that date back to the days of kings. They will also explain why products made in Austria are the best in the world.

The people of Austria have a deep-rooted respect for wildlife and the outdoors. They have preserved their country and their heritage. They deserve our admiration and respect.

Going to Turkey Camp

- Missouri

The road stretched on forever but I didn't see it. I was aware only of the continuous whirring sound of my tires on the road. My subconscious held the truck between the stripes aiming it around slower vehicles. The radio was cranked up and the pounding beat of classic rock sparked my internal engine driving me forward. The speedometer indicated my desires outweighed good sense. I had one purpose – to get away from a stifling social order to the rejuvenating life of hunting camp. I was escaping.

Dark clouds bulged from the sky like chocolate clabber milk ready to spill. Then a surprising bolt of lightening made me jerk and blink. A quick thunderstorm drenched the world for a few minutes, and stopped. Mother Nature was letting me know what she could do if she ever made up her mind.

My canvas spike tent, a stove, lanterns, ice chest, shovel, saw, and axe were in the bed of the truck. Everything that needed to stay dry was stacked in the cab. My hunting boots were on the passenger floorboard. My clothes bag, various jackets, and a hunting cap were on the seat. There was also my grandpa's twin-hammered double-barreled 12-gauge shotgun.

Years ago, when we were starting our lives, there were hunting camps scattered throughout the county. Each camp was filled with expert liars and prophets. Wood stoves heated ramshackle camp houses while old cardboard boxes provided insulation. Discarded second-hand tin served as a roof, and similar plywood made a good floor.

The best time to be in one of these camps was the night before deer season. It was better than Christmas.

Some camps consisted of families. But the camps that held my interest were the ones that were only men. The hard simple roughness, ribald stories, abundant beverages, and poker games hypnotized me and branded my soul.

These camps stood far back from the graveled farm roads. Most of them were tucked into thickets or concealed in cavernous deep woods. A person had to know their site to locate them. Others were at the end of an oil field road and a half-dozen gates needed opening and closing to find their sanctuary.

Now, they are gone. The graveled roads have been paved and connect every destination in a ridiculous spider web of convenience. Most of the old-timers have died. The land was inherited and split between daughters and lard-butted mama's boys who would rather sleep in the fat comfort of their own beds than a cot in hunting camp. Society stole my church.

My foot got heavier and the truck picked up speed as I crossed state lines. The world outside my cab was, for a short time, an insignificant blur. However, when the geography began to change I started watching the scenery.

One of my compadres, Clint Dalbom, invited me to turkey camp in southern Missouri. He has some yada-yada-not-quite-a-big-whig job with the state conservation department and it seemed logical he should have the primo turkey hunting locales nailed.

I cannonballed off the interstate and had to slow down when I turned on a state highway. Then I followed Clint's directions to a narrow snaking two lane.

Speed lost its urgency. The green rolling hills and immaculate landscaped farmsteads captivated my attention. Bright floral colors and the awareness of fresh air awakened my senses and further impeded my progress. Newborn colts, lambs, and calves danced in the springtime fields experimenting with life, but staying near their mothers. An old rusted pickup chugged towards me and we both eased over to allow passage. At the appropriate distance I waved, and the other driver waved back. At once, all the gunk built up within me disappeared and I felt washed and clean.

Clint, and his buddy Bill, met me at the designated rendezvous. We hooted our howdys, exchanged handshakes and backslapping, and cussed each other with fitting names. When the revelry of the moment subsided we hurried back to our rigs and I dropped in behind him for the remainder of the trip. Now, we were on a gravel road.

Camp was everything I expected. It was a functional layout of exponential genius. There were two cattle trailers, serving as sleeping quarters, covered with blue plastic tarps. A fire smoldered in a ring of large rocks centralizing all activities. A kitchen cabinet stood beside a trailer. Propane bottles, lanterns, and cook stoves were within handy reach. A short walk from the hub of this backwoods Mecca was a Wal-Mart lawn chair with hole cut in the seat. It was backed against a tree with a strategic hole dug underneath.

Ten male disciples of turkey camp inhabited the trailers. They were all related through the aristocratic pedigreed bloodline of the tobacco spitting gobbler seekers, and they recognized me as a long lost cousin.

Each hunter injected his unique personality into the camp. They covered the spectrum of employment from carpenters to desk jockeys. They were no silly kids. All these men understood their modern-day responsibilities, but they also knew how to leave the pressures of the daily grind behind and appreciate the outdoors.

They gathered for a common cause. The foremost reason was to be in turkey camp, and then running a close second was to hunt turkeys. Boyhood memories flickered through my mind as I listened to lies around the campfire and became saturated with the scent of woodsmoke. I languished, absorbing the hunting tips offered by my new buddies, listening to the laughter, and relishing the sincerity of my surroundings. The night sky was clouded and devoid of moonlight, but the kindred hearts of the hunters shined through their smiles and voices.

The long hours of driving finally tagged me and I retired to my tent and bedroll. The woodland night peepers sang their lullaby, and I slept like a dead man.

Camp woke long before the sun came up. Clint came to my tent and rousted me up. Everyone was moving around by lantern light. They were dressed in their camo-uniforms, and there was a general sleepy excitement of getting out for the first morning.

Clint and I headed for a ridge he had scouted previously. A rocky-bottomed creek lent its musical tinkling to the darkness. Then far off, Clint heard a turkey gobble. He pointed in its direction and we hurried off the ridge.

We set up in a meadow below the hill. Clint situated his decoy and I moved ahead to hide beneath a cedar tree. In a few moments, Clint began to cluck and putt like a turkey hen. I listened and tried to imagine all the sounds I'd heard so many years ago around a farmyard.

The gobbler answered. Then there was another, and another. We waited and the anticipation grew. Clint continued the yelping serenade. Then he made a noise like a jake.

In a moment, the gobblers appeared. There were three of them. They were headed in our direction. They came at a trot, then stopped, and one of them strutted and beat his wings. Then they all three galumphed down the hill towards us.

My double-barrel rested on my knees pointing straight out in front of me. All they had to do was walk by. I was motionless, but my pulse throbbed in my throat and my cold hands began to sweat.

The gobblers wobbled towards us. The distance was closing; another 20 yards and I'd have a shot.

Then somewhere behind me a coyote barked. Clint clucked his lovesick hen cadence, but the gobblers froze. Then they walked deliberately, changing directions, and circled us – out of shooting range. There was nothing we could do but watch them leave.

We followed the chorus of gobblers all over the oak-covered hills the rest of the morning, but it wasn't meant to be.

Our return to camp was met by similar stories from the other hunters. Nobody had filled a tag the opening morning. But nobody complained. Everyone was just happy to be in turkey camp.

The next day was practically a repeat of the first. By the end of the third hunt there was only one unlucky short-bearded bird in camp.

Still, none of the hunters complained. We all spent our days pussyfooting through the wooded hills of the Missouri countryside, enjoying the beauty of the dogwoods, in tune with our natural surroundings, and trying to outsmart the dumb homely gamebirds.

Despite the lack of feathers on the meatpole, camp was our gratifying home. Each hunter had his turn reliving the adventures of the day, and each hunter loved hearing the others' tales.

Camp did not exist without its mishaps. I burned a hole in the top of my tent. Other hunters suffered embarrassing missed opportunities. But next year, when the hard disciplined hand of society seems like it's become too much to bear – we'll all be going back to turkey camp.

Valuable Moments
and Memories

- Wyoming

S ometimes special moments come and go and we don't realize what we've experienced until the event is long past. It's good fortune when we have the opportunity to live in a dream, realize it – and make it last.

The weather was perfect. The daily sunshine raised the temperature into the low 70s. The night sky was dense blackness littered with millions of piercing silver stars and complimented by a growing moon. The nights tingled with frost.

We slept tucked away in our bedrolls in the crew tent. There were six of us piled into the tent and it had a "kids at camp" sort of feeling. We never went to sleep without a round of jokes or practical pranks.

The crew was the most competent I've ever worked with. The cook always had a smile and made sure that everyone was staying fat and happy. The wrangler never dodged a chore and showed obvious enthusiasm. The other guides were all experienced in one fashion or another. They had either hunted the area or had enough knowledge of guiding that they were capable of handling the job.

The outfitter, Todd Jones, was an educated fellow who understood human needs and tendencies. He worked with a pleasant attitude and always had a quick grin and witty remark for any situation.

The camp was laid out across 100 yards along the creek bottom, the cook tent being the focal point of interest. The other tents were scattered between the pine trees and spaced at distances that gave the set-up a sense of privacy – yet openness. A single foot trail was the connecting vein.

The camp was also the least labor intensive I'd ever seen. Propane heaters and abundant grass eliminated the need for spending countless hours chopping wood and packing hay. A short five-mile ride from the trailhead makes the outside world more accessible.

The horses and mules were also a pleasure to work with. The guest's horses were old campaigners that knew their work. The mules were all short, easy to pack, and had good dispositions.

The hunting was phenomenal. This was a resident wilderness elk herd. They winter in the same place they live the rest of the year. The demographics of the herd population are perfect. There are a dozen drainages within an easy ride from camp. Every drainage holds a group of elk consisting of a herd bull with four to twelve cows and half-a-dozen satellite bulls. Then there are the spikes that run around acting lost and the raghorn bulls that are waiting their turn to fight for dominance. Our hunting area covered more than 30 square miles and it was impossible to ride down the valley without hearing the challenge of bugling bulls.

There is also an abundance of grizzlies – just as there should be.

The country was simple to learn. Every drainage spread up from the creek bottom and turned into an open ridge, covered with grass, that extended like a bony finger to the snow-coated peaks.

We had the valley to ourselves for the first eight-day hunt of the archery season. The outfitter admitted we were having a banner year. The constant bugling kept our hunters awake at night.

Each day the hunters and guides had new stories to tell about their close encounters with elk. A cow brushed one hunter aside as a bull chased her. A spike came within inches of stepping on a hunter as the hunter watched with amused anticipation. One hunter had to hunt for a wounded bull only to find it buried by a grizzly.

Out of the group of five hunters, only one never released an arrow. He was the class woodsman who refused to shoot unless a clean killing shot was one hundred percent positive.

The week was like a dream. It was unbelievable. Archery hunters were passing on good bulls wanting bigger ones. We were all living in paradise. The hunting was from an elk hunter's fairy tale book, but we all knew we needed to savor the experience.

My hunter collected a fine 5x5 bull the first morning at 8:15. We spent the rest of the week flyfishing for trout and enjoying life in the Wyoming mountains.

A Hard Road Trip to New Knowledge and Adventure

- Wyoming

Anxiety frayed my nerves. My three bay horses trotted into the pen and found their places in individual stalls. They were obnoxious and cute, like rowdy young boys, as they displayed their impatience. My pulse pounded in my temples and I was aggravated while pouring grain in each feed box. Then I stepped back, watched them eat, and the sight settled me. I stood and admired my favorite four-legged companions. I was homesick before my trip started.

The plan was to leave at midnight. I was going to Wyoming to guide elk hunters for an outfitter I'd never met, in country I'd never seen - and I was skeptical. It gets harder to leave home and loved ones every year.

I loaded my truck in the dark, grumbling while I stacked the hunting gear. Then I cussed when I heaved the saddle to the top of the pile. For a silent moment I stood looking at the object I married so long ago, the working tool that identified me and cursed me to a bittersweet lifestyle. Then I shook my head and a small part of me surrendered to my scheduled task.

I woke my daughter and hugged her before I left then tucked her into the bedcovers. She muttered a dreamy "I Love You Daddy," and slipped back into her peaceful slumber. Another bigger part of me cried deep inside.

The new cattle guard didn't rattle when I pulled out of the gravel driveway and steered the truck towards the pavement. I left Shaws Bend resolved to the long drive. I gunned past La Grange, Waco, Fort Worth, Wichita Falls, and Vernon.

Childress, Texas is one of my landmarks. I turned the corner into the Panhandle and smiled when I passed the center of town with its statue of a saddle. Hours later I sailed out of the state at Texline. I was in cowboy country.

I was catching gears and yawning while hopping over Raton Pass and by the time I reached Denver I needed a pot of coffee. Then I crossed into Wyoming and the world of farmers and civilized corporate folks began to disappear in my rearview mirror

- and I didn't look back. I was cruising. Then at Casper, I drifted northwest.

A few hours later, I started suffering road founder. My mind shut down blank and numb. The cab of the truck was a cockpit filled with junk except for the cubbyhole behind the wheel. I was a pilot blaring across the Red Desert, tight and snug oblivious to the world I was rocketing through. My burning eyes were stuck open - staring.

I reached for the radio when nearing the Wind River Reservation and hit a station that was playing Indian music. This wasn't the dope smoking flute music they sell at the mall and pass off as Indian music. This was war drums and deep guttural chants that make the hair on the back of your neck stand up. It makes your gut tight, your skin crawl, and makes you start cleaning your guns. War drums reverberated off the interior of my airtight capsule, and I turned the volume up.

I started believing I could understand the primal drum-beating chorus. My imagination took over. I was in camp, sitting by the fire, and then crab-crawling backwards into the shadows with my pistols and knife ready for an attack.

Then a chilling reality jerked me awake. I did understand something they said. I turned the volume louder. There it was barely discernable in a morose monotone Indian anthem.

*"Mickey Mouse, Minnie Mouse, Pluto too... they're all movie stars at Disneyland!"

I almost wrecked the truck. The words repeated themselves another dozen times and I figured I'd finally gone crazy. The station turned into static and I drove on in silence bewildered by what I thought I'd heard.

Then, my brain shifted to an old way of thinking. I no longer looked for road signs. Instead, I looked for mountains and a place to turn due north. I began looking for a river or some concourse of topography to follow. Somehow my befuddled instincts knew that beyond the Red Desert, some distance from the well-traveled concrete and asphalt, was the Washakie Wilderness and the rendezvous with the outfitter. I was getting the itch only my saddle could satisfy. I wanted to leave the fetters of society.

I was headed to a new job, with new hunting grounds, and new people. There were new mountains to climb, new creeks to cross, new trails to follow, and though I still ached for the folks I left at home - I was headed to a new adventure.

---

* English lyrics are used as a tool for young Indians learning how the songs of their heritage were written.

Suggested Outfitters

This listing of outfitters is no deviant step away from storytelling toward commercialism. It is an honest effort to introduce folks who have befriended me and given a saddle bum a job when times were hard.

For the reader, picking an outfitter is harder than picking your kinfolks. The men and women I've worked for are solid people. Different regions offer varying degrees of quality hunting, fishing, and outdoor experiences. Some are luxury resorts while others supply the finest wilderness camps in some of the wildest backcountry in North America.

All of them are at the top of their game supplying good cooks, warm dry places to sleep, and conscientious efforts to satisfy your expectations.

Luxury resorts include:

Mexico	~ to ~	Montana

Hacienda Don Quixote	H Lazy 6 Ranch
The Adventure Group	Hank and Laura Bouma
Don Turner	P.O. Box 971
P.O. Box 608	Choteau, Montana 59422
McAllen, Texas 78505	www.hlazy6ranch.com
www.viphunts.com	

The Bob Marshall Wilderness is high country heaven on earth spraddled across two million mountainous acres. Your heart will whisper you're headed towards adventure every time you straddle a horse and ride up the trail into the timber. It offers countless photographic opportunities including the Chinese Wall, Gates Park, Headquarters Pass, Sock Lake, Gateway Gorge, and the Sleeping Buffalo. The fly fishing along the Sun River can make a novice look like an expert. However, when a hunter packs an elk out of the "Bob," he's damn sure earned it. And there is no finer way to live than in a primitive elk camp with the men and women of the wilderness. Suggested camps include:

7 Lazy P Guest Ranch	Montana Safaris	A Lazy H Outfitters
Chuck & Sharon Blixrud	Rocky & Lorel Heckman	Al & Sally Haas
P.O. Box 178	21 Airport Road	P.O. Box 1079
Choteau, Mt. 59422	Choteau, Mt. 59422	Choteau, Mt. 59422

Wyoming, likewise, offers some of the most scenic beauty in America. State laws and accessibility have prohibited the plundering of many of its natural resources.

Here resides an outfitter who, in my estimation, is one of the best of the best.

Todd Jones
Paintrock Adventures
P.O. Box 52
Hyattville, Wyoming 82428
www.paintrock.com

Todd's summer camp is a superb layout in the Cloud Peak Wilderness, and he knows the fishing holes wherein await magnificent golden trout. His crew is an amazing collection of college degreed experts who can pack an elk, write a thesis, give fly fishing lessons, or snap out a home-cooked meal from a dutch oven. Then, for a wilderness camp, his elk hunting is phenomenal.

Booking a hunt for Texas or Mexico white-tailed deer can be aggravating. Again, trying to find a reputable outfitter who can produce what they promise is an impractical chore. The hunts are overpriced, unless, you figure in the cost of the private sector management. All these hunts are on somebody's ranch. Often, an outfitter is a third party selling a deer. Then there are booking agents, supplemental feeding, guide costs, equipment costs, and food costs.

When booking a hunt, the buyer has to question whether they're paying to "hunt" or paying to "shoot." This is the land of open range, canned hunts, and every varying degree in between. The buyer must decide what is acceptable in their universe of sportsmanship.

However, every chunk of country holds its own spectacular colors of nature. The cactus brush country, with its javelina, rattlesnakes, road runners, and muy grande bucks, is yet another place to appreciate the opportunity of seeing what God made for man to enjoy.

The outfitter suggested is a good consultant, and an upright young man surrounded by a strong support crew of family and friends. He also has some great dove hunting.

Mexico Outfitters Unlimited

Clay Young
P.O.B. 421374
Del Rio, Texas 78842

Yaupon Notes

Yaupon Notes

Yaupon Notes

Yaupon Notes

Yaupon Notes

Yaupon Notes

www.ingramcontent.com/pod-product-compliance
Lightning Source LLC
Chambersburg PA
CBHW062052270326
41931CB00013B/3048